p6

APR 2004

The Legends & Lands of
Native North Americans

DAVID MARTÍNEZ, Ph.D.

Photography by ELAN PENN

Sterling Publishing Co., Inc. New York
A Sterling/Penn Book

Edited by Jeanette Green

Designed by Spinning Egg Design Group, Inc.

Cartography by Michel Opatowski

Library of Congress Cataloging-in-Publication Data
Martinez, David, 1963–
The legends & lands of Native North Americans / David Martinez ;
photography by Elan Penn.
p. cm.
Includes bibliographical references and index.
ISBN 1-4027-0411-9
1. Indians of North America--Folklore. 2. Tales--United States.
3. Indians of North America--Social life and customs. I. Title: Legends and
Lands of Native North Americans. II. Penn, Elan. III. Title.
E98.F6M27 2003
398.2'089'97--dc21

2003000288

1 3 5 7 9 10 8 6 4 2

Published by Sterling Publishing Co., Inc.
387 Park Avenue South, New York, N.Y. 10016

Penn Publishing, Ltd. 20 Hatichon St.,
P.O. Box 2190, Savyon, Israel 56530
© 2003 by Penn Publishing, Ltd.
Distributed in Canada by Sterling Publishing
ᶜ/o Canadian Manda Group, One Atlantic Avenue, Suite 105
Toronto, Ontario, Canada M6K 3E7
Distributed in Great Britain by Chrysalis Books
64 Brewery Road, London N7 9NT, England
Distributed in Australia by Capricorn Link (Australia) Pty. Ltd.
P.O. Box 704, Windsor, NSW 2756 Australia

Printed in China

ISBN 1-4027-0411-9

Cover photo: Bighorn National Forest, Wyoming

In memory of Martin Martínez,
loving father and life-long denizen of the West

In memory of my dear father, Isar Penn,
who gave me my first camera

Contents

Preface

The Native American stories in this book come from a variety of sources, both told and new. I compiled them from the abundant wealth of myth and legend anthologies created by such luminaries as Elsie Clews Parsons, Ella Clark, Frances Densmore, George Bird Grinnell, Henry Schoolcraft, Richard Erodoes, and Alfonso Ortiz, to name a few. The study of American Indian mythology has become a very sophisticated field in which analyzing texts is as important as the oral tradition itself.

If we are fortunate enough, we may still be able to hear these stories being told today. American Indian oral tradition is far from extinct. Although the oral tradition depends, perhaps precariously, on the memories of people who may be old and whose communities may be struggling to maintain native languages, the need for these stories remains the same. The stories are told to account for why a given people were meant to live in a particular land. They are told to account for the origins of clans and ceremonies. They are told to explain why there is death and suffering as well as why kinship and laughter are important. Stories are even told to pass the time away.

As for myself, I tell these stories in the courses I teach in American Indian Studies. Both Indian and non-Indian students take these classes. Consequently, different students hear or see different things in each of the tales I spin. But what all my students have in common is a natural capacity to understand these stories in their own personal terms. Unlike theory, a story appeals to the individual; it beckons him onto the narrative's path. Once he is on this path, the story becomes his own journey. At the end of the tale (or should I say trail?) there awaits enlightenment, direction, even healing. But one can only attain these things if he is willing to believe in them.

Collected in this book are stories still handed down among the Indian nations of the Southwest, Great Plains, Northeast, and Northwest. I have written them in the same fashion that I tell them myself—in my own words but without unnecessary embellishment. I remain true to the events and themes of the original oral stories, so that the spirit of each legend is retained.

1

WHEN THE WORLD WAS
VERY YOUNG

Traveling across North America means encountering both the lives and ghosts of Indian people. From the Adirondacks to Vancouver Island and from the Black Hills to the Four Corners, Indians still command prominent places across the continent.

As Americans, wherever we go, we cross land that was either historically or spiritually important to Indian communities. After all, there is more to Indian Country than what you find on reservations. The signs of the people are everywhere. If you begin your journey in the east, however, it is easy to suppose that Indians are no more than a memory, a vanished people whose traces are merely place names on a road map. Belying such an image are the Indian communities that endure and even flourish in various parts of New England, New York, and Ontario, such as the Iroquois, the Penobscot, and the Passamaquoddy. Farther west, the presence of Indian people becomes more obvious in places like South Dakota, Wyoming, and Montana, where you can find thriving communities of Dakota, Cheyenne, and Crow. Upon reaching the Pacific Northwest, we find the Kwakiutl, Nootka, and Salishan peoples of Vancouver Island and the Olympic Peninsula. Then, of course, the Southwest remains an important focal point for anyone seeking cultures that are as old as time. Off the main highways, we find Navajo, Hopi, and Pueblo peoples, such as the Acoma and Zuñi, still inhabiting the same places recounted in legend.

This book invites you to journey to the origin of these places. Of course, there are far too many places and origin stories to cover than is possible in a single volume like this one. Nevertheless, long before North America became the United States, Canada, and Mexico, it was Turtle Island and the Glittering World, among other names. Rather than a nation-state, this continent was host to a broad range of homelands, from woodlands to prairies to deserts.

Each of these places inspired an epic creation story, each time told in a different language. In fact, when you listen to Indian legends you soon realize that they are rich in the details and ambiance of *where* they are told. While reading the legends contained in this volume, remember that they *happened* in the places captured in the photographs. These legends do not take place in a mythical or theoretical domain. They take place in *this* world, beneath your feet. The relationship between Indians and their homelands, then, is one that is based on legendary phenomena. The stories do not disclose a history but an eternal bond between the destinies of peoples and the places that were created for them.

Throughout these legends are recurrent features that fully define the relationship between people and place. First, the land is always a *gift* that was created especially for a certain people, making the people in a sense *chosen* by their creator. "In ancient time," for example, the Arikara believe that "the Great Spirit Above sent Mother Corn" to them. She would be a source of health and strength. "She has walked with our people," the Arikara affirm, "on the long and difficult path they have traveled from the faraway past, and now she marches with us toward the future." Second, the land, including its animals and plants, always determines the kind of customs and beliefs a people follow.

The Salishan people tell a story of Old-One, who created the world, and who made the people from balls of mud. Unfortunately, the people were not very knowledgeable. So, Old-One sent them Coyote for a teacher. "Old-One told Coyote," the legend goes, "to teach Indians the best way to do things and the best way to make things." Life would be much easier for them, as it turned out, when they listened to Coyote.

Third, the kinds of spirits a people believe in are the spirits that inhabit the land itself. The Hopis speak of a Wind God who lives inside a crater in Sunset Mountain, while the Zuñi tell a story about a hummingbird who was also a man, and who married a beautiful young woman.

Fourth, it is these spirits of the land that will teach the people, perhaps through a particular culture hero, how to get food, shelter, and medicine from the land. For the Kwakiutl, Wakiash brought them totem poles and masked dances by visiting the animal people in a vision.

Last, a people's notion of being healthy, happy, and successful is derived from the land. In the legend of the Night Chant, a Navajo hunter called The Dreamer was taught this healing ceremony as a reward for his restraint when confronted with four mountain sheep. The sheep were really *yeis*, powerful spirits. The yeis transformed themselves and The Dreamer into mountain sheep, after which they traveled for four days before arriving at a hogan made with white shell, turquoise, abalone, and jet. Within the hogan a ceremony was performed, during which "The Dreamer paid careful attention to all the songs, prayers, paintings, and dance movements....When the chant was over, he had

Nimpkish Burial Grounds, Alert Bay, British Columbia

learned all the details of the....*Kieje Hatal*, the 'Night Chant'." Such a ceremony would enable the Navajo to maintain *hózhó* in their lives, which is their word for beauty, harmony, order, and goodness.

Everything begins with a story, and the story itself often begins in total darkness, because the sun and moon have yet to be created. Within the darkness there may be either a vast ocean or an endless void, for the earth does not yet exist. This is the time before time when spirits would wander about, suddenly getting the urge to create something. Maybe they were lonely. Maybe they needed light and beauty. Or perhaps they just needed someplace to call home. According to the Crow, before Old Man Coyote proceeded to create the world, he thought to himself: "It is bad that I am alone. I should have someone to talk to. It is bad that there is only water and nothing else."

Before there were people, though, there was the land. The Mandans tell a creation story in which there were two persons who created the earth, First Creator and Lone Man. First Creator made a land filled with beautiful landscapes of "broad valleys, hills, coulees with timber, mountain streams, springs," as well as "the buffalo elk, black-tailed and white-tailed antelope, mountain sheep, and all other creatures useful to mankind for food and clothing." Lone Man, on the other hand, created a very different land that was flat for the most part, containing lakes, small streams, and rivers that were far apart. Lone Man also created the beaver, otter, and muskrat, as well as different colored cattle with long horns and long tails. The Mandans would use both types of land over time, as it was meant to be.

*Wikaninnish Bay, Pacific Rim
National Park, Washington*

In many cases you find that the earth's creators were meticulous in the work that they did. When First Man and First Woman created Mount Taylor, they called it *Tzo dsil*, and it was one of the six sacred mountains that encompass the *Dinétah*, the Navajo homeland. Mount Taylor, in particular, was made "from the soil that First Man had gathered from the mountains in the Third World"—one of the worlds that existed below the present world—and which First Man "kept in his medicine bag." Some of the things that made this mountain sacred were the "turquoise, white corn, dark mists, and female rain" which First Man and First Woman were careful to use in adorning this place.

Canyon de Chelly National Monument, Arizona

Such examples make clear that the land is more than where a story took place, it is a story in its own right. Because when you look at a place, you are seeing something happen. This becomes more apparent when you accept the land, including plants and animals, as a form of conscious life, complete with memory and intelligence. Throughout countless Indian legends, it is not only animals that can speak but even the rocks and trees. Everything in nature then becomes a part of the stories that Indian people hand down through the generations.

Stockade Lake, Custer State Park, South Dakota

Do animals tell stories? Not exactly. But they do pass along to their offspring a way of doing things that is not written down. Indians also have a way of doing things that is free from the confines of the text. Whereas animals may inherit from their parents the instincts they need to survive, Indian people inherit from their elders the symbols that organize their cultural world into a meaningful whole.

At one level, then, as Paul Zolbrod claims in *Reading the Voice*, creation stories, insofar as they may be regarded as a form of "poetry," are "fundamental to what emerges as a poetic tradition of a people, which predicates what lies at the heart of all that emerges palpably as their culture." But these stories are more than literature, let alone a mere genre; they are the foundation of culture itself, stemming from the most basic and fundamental experiences required for founding a people. It is because these stories are paramount that they not only go back to "mythic" time but also to the time *before* there were humans.

"When the world was very young, there were no people on the earth," states a Makah story. "A very long time ago," says a Hopi legend, "there was nothing but water on the earth." Among the Navajo, they tell a story that "begins in a small world bordered on all four sides with ocean. It is populated by insect people."

Petroglyphs, Mesa Verde
National Park, Colorado

The time of these stories is when the animals could speak. Even when the stories tell about the adventures of humans, they are not quite the same people you meet everyday. Because of this, many Indian languages make a distinction between legends that are about the times before and after the creation of ordinary people. The Coeur d'Alene, as Rodney Frey observes in *Stories That Made the World*, "call the narratives about the myth people, *me-y-mi-ym qesp schint*, roughly translated 'he/she is going to tell stories about the time before human beings'." The Western Apache, in turn, refer to myths as stories that occurred "'in the beginning' (*godiyaaná*), a time," according to Keith Basso, "when the universe and all things within it were achieving their present form and location."

Then there are the Ojibwe who speak of myths, *ätíso'kanak*, which are sacred stories that may only be told during certain times of the year, usually winter. "The significant thing about these stories," according to A. Irving Hallowell, "is that the characters in them are regarded as living entities who have existed from time immemorial." This means that the mythical Thunderbirds are as real as the hawks and eagles that can be spotted in Ojibwe country. Moreover, it is the case that the stories are living entities as well; they have a life of their own insofar as these stories continue to be told.

In other words, the oral tradition has more in common with nature than with the artificiality of writing. This becomes apparent in the Lakota account of Thunderbirds. The *Wakinyan*, the Thunderbird, is a powerful being who hates all that is "dirty" but loves everything that is "clean and pure." According to legend, there are actually four Thunderbirds, dominating each of the four directions. The most prominent Thunderbird is the one from the west. "He is clothed in clouds," according to one account. "His body has no form, but he has giant, four-jointed wings. He has no feet, but enormous claws. He has no head, but a huge, sharp beak with rows of big, pointed teeth." Each Thunderbird's home, in turn, is guarded by a specific animal. The home of the west is protected by a bear; the north by a deer; the east by a butterfly; and the south by a beaver.

When you take such legends into consideration, it may finally dawn on you that the reason why Indians do not feel a compulsion to leave many symbols of their presence across the land is because nature itself is already full of meaning. Everything is a part of a story. You only need to look and remember.

When you look at the photos in this book, you will see grandeur, the powers of the earth, and beauty. However, you will not in many cases detect any evidence of people. Indeed, you may see what explorers and frontiersmen saw when they laid their eyes on America for the first

Black Hills National Forest, South Dakota

time—nothing. For what may not be readily apparent when looking at the places Indians call home is that a place may actually belong to a people with barely a sign that they were ever there. A place may even be eminently sacred without so much as a fence around it to distinguish it from the rest of "wild" nature. Consequently, a particular glade, butte, mesa, or river bend may be where a

sacred being once stood, however, there will not be any plaques or statues, let alone houses of worship, there to turn what was a mythical event into a monument.

What is just a cave for most may actually be where some Cheyenne found a pathway to the prairies where they discovered the buffalo. Or, what looks like no more than a rocky spire in the middle of a canyon floor could be where Spider Woman helped a young Navajo escape from an approaching enemy.

For those of us who are accustomed to sacred places being marked by grand structures, like the Wailing Wall or the Dome of the Rock, leaving such sites to blend in with the rest of the environment may be difficult to understand. It becomes more difficult to comprehend when you come from a tradition in which land is not only a form of property, but also whose value cannot be appreciated unless it is "developed" or "exploited" in some way. After all, a place is yours if you have invested it with your own labor, such as through farming, mining, or cattle ranching. "This is *my* land," as John Wayne claimed as a Texas rancher in *Red River*, regardless of any prior claims made by Mexicans or Comanches. Without such an investment, can you really claim a place that remains as natural as when God created it? For Indians the answer is yes. And it is a valid response when you accept the premise that the only true "owner" of the land is the One who created it.

Monument Valley Navajo Tribal Park, Arizona

It is not simply that individuals are mortal while the land is everlasting—though that is a part of it—rather, even a whole tribe cannot claim to own a place in the western sense of the term. No one can. This is so because the people were not given the *right* to dispose of the land as they saw fit. On the contrary, what they were *given* was the *responsibility* to maintain the integrity of their homeland as it was created for them. Indians would do this by keeping to the

path that their ancestors established for them, which is recounted in their legends. As Chief Joseph said on behalf of the Nez Percés' claim to the Wallowa Valley: "The earth was created by the assistance of the sun, and it should be left as it was....The country was made without lines of demarcation, and it is no man's business to divide it....The earth and myself are of one mind. The measure of the land and the measure of our bodies are the same."

Separating yourself from the land, whether by choice or by force, means cutting yourself off from life itself and all that was good in your world. Araphooish captured the urgency of this relationship when he said on behalf of the Crow: "The Crow Country is a good country. The Great Spirit put it exactly in the right place; while you are in it, you fare well; whenever you are out of it, whichever way you travel, you fare worse."

Be they Navajo, Kwakiutl, Lakota, or Micmac, a people "belong" to a given place in the same manner that a family belongs to their home. But a home in Indian Country is something that you *share* with other creatures. Animals, heroes, and forces of nature were there first to set the stage for human occupation. Indeed, you almost get the sense that humans did not need to be created at all; certainly not for the sake of dominating the world. Instead, humans were created for the same reason that all the plants and animals were created—because it was *possible* to create them. People are merely a part of the exfoliation of Life.

In the Makah creation story they talk of a time when there were no birds, animals, or people. Aside from the grass and sand, there were "creatures that were neither animals nor people but had some of the traits of people and some of the traits of animals." These would become all the living beings of the earth. In light of this, perhaps another way of understanding the relation between people and

The Mittens, Monument Valley
Navajo Tribal Park, Arizona

homeland is by considering the example of the animals. A people belong to a homeland in the way that bees belong to their hive or bears to their den. Home is an integral part of a people's identity. It is as much a part of who they are as knowing their relatives and speaking the same language.

It would be the animals' example, after all, that would form the bases of many of the traditions practiced by Indian people. Among the Sanpoil of the Pacific Northwest, for example, it was Coyote who taught the people how to catch and treat the salmon that would be the mainstay of their diet. Coyote did this because he wanted a certain beautiful girl for his wife, so he set out to impress her grandparents, Old Man and Old Woman. After Coyote fixed Old Man's traps, Old Man was overjoyed to see that they had caught many salmon. The first thing that Coyote did was take one of the salmon over to a flat place on the ground, where he placed it on a bed of sunflower stems and leaves. Coyote then instructed Old Man on how to properly prepare salmon for eating, as well as what to do with the salmon's bones. The most important thing was to save the back part of the head for a sacred bundle. "If you do as I tell you," Coyote asserted, "you will always have plenty of salmon in your trap." The consequences, however, for violating these instructions meant risking death. So, Old Man continued to do as he was shown, and soon the rest of the people noticed his success. After inviting the people to a salmon feast, Old Man and Old Woman shared the lessons of Coyote with them, after which the way of Coyote became the Sanpoil way.

The struggle for survival is a common theme among countless Indian legends. Famine, war, and disease are more than mere literary themes—they are the ways in which a people earn their right to a given homeland. What we sometimes forget is that creating a homeland takes generations of struggle and learning, the fruit of which is handed down to a people's children. What they inherit through these legends are the dialogues with life and death that inspired people to seek sources of knowledge beyond the everyday world. What they often return with is a story, which is really an experience. Christopher Vecsey observes about Indian legends in *Imagine Ourselves Richly*:

"They represent situations in which boundaries have been crossed—from unconsciousness to consciousness, innocence to experience, natural to cultural, chaos to order—not just any liminal crossings, however, but thresholds that have made a life-and-death difference to humanity."

Custer State Park, South Dakota

Sometimes the story is about earning the right to hunt a particular animal. There was a time, for example, according to the Cheyenne, when the buffalo would eat humans. That only changed when all the animals held a race around Devils Tower. Many animals raced until they dropped dead on the ground, and their blood can still be seen in the red dirt surrounding this landmark. Humans won only with the help of magpie and hawk, both of whom raced on the side of people. From that day forward, humans hunted buffalo. At other times, a sacrifice was necessary, such as in the Penobscot and Passamaquoddy story about the origin of corn and tobacco.

Klos-kur-beh, the Great Teacher, lived where no peopled dwelled. Klos-kur-beh, however, would always go to the people when they were in peril. Indeed, he was there from the beginning when the first

Painted Desert, Petrified Forest National Park, Arizona

man and first woman were created. They would be the first to approach Klos-kur-beh for help. They would go to his solitary home in the "Northland," where he was always waiting for the next time his people needed him. One of those times was during a famine. First Mother and her husband did not know what to do to feed their children, which left First Mother despondent. After seeking Klos-kur-beh's counsel, the husband was told to do whatever his wife asked of him. Upon returning with these instructions, First Mother told her husband to slay her, then drag her body back and forth across an open field. Once there was nothing left of her body but bones, they should bury these in the middle of the field. After seven months, something would grow that the people could harvest. With the aid of two other men, the husband did as his wife asked him. What they found seven months later were tall, beautiful plants that they called *Skar-mu-nal*, or Corn, and a plant that had bitter leaves, which they named Utar-*mur-wa-yeh*, or Tobacco. Because of the sacred origins of these plants, Klos-kur-beh gave the people special instructions on how to respect these sacred plants. "And since these things came from the goodness of a woman's heart," the Great Teacher said, "see that you hold her always in memory. Remember her when you eat. Remember her when the smoke of her bones rises before you....Let all share alike, for so will the love of the First Mother have been fulfilled."

As stories like these clearly indicate, when Indians engage in all the activities that make up their traditional lives, from eating corn, smoking tobacco, or hunting a great animal, they are perpetuating cultures that are indebted to the life-and-death struggles of ancestors. For all the substances of the earth are mixed with the blood of those who came before. Remembering and retelling their stories therefore is an act of commemoration, in the sense of being a ceremony through which communal bonds are renewed. Moreover, for most Indians, ancestors live on in the ceremonies that serve as the cornerstones in the people's lives.

For the Hopi of the Southwest, what lies beyond the impermanence of this world is the Skeleton House. The Hopi learned of this place because a certain young man began to wonder what became of the dead. Since the young man was sincere in his quest for knowledge, Badger Old Man gave him medicine that enabled him to virtually die and see the fate of the dead for himself. What he found along the way were people traveling paths that were either difficult or easy depending on how well they followed the Hopi path of life while they were still living. Upon reaching the Skeleton House, he saw spirits as light as air, who fed only on the odor of solid food.

What the young man learned from these skeleton people was that the living must work for the dead. By that they meant that the Hopi must continue with their ceremonies, with everything that makes up the Hopi way. In return, the Skeleton House people would work for the living by sending them rain and crops. The young man returned to the living with the knowledge he gained from his visit. He then told the people what he saw and learned. "Very well," they conceded, "very well; so that is the way." With that the people returned to their homes wiser than before. Thus, the Hopi way continues for as long as they honor their dead, who are really the kachinas, who make the earth sustain the lives of the people, for the kachinas are inherent in the earth itself.

From the starry heavens above to the earth below, and onward to the land of the dead, Indians know the extent of their homelands. Their boundaries were established not by surveyors applying the homogenous forms of geometry to the land; rather, they emerged out of the collective experiences of the people. Boundaries extend to where they know how to get food; where they can reach safety; where they can communicate with sacred beings; and where they can go for medicine. Because the land is vast, sometimes different people will all lay claims to the same place. The Lakota, Cheyenne, and Kiowa, for example, all have legends about Devils Tower. Each claim is valid because Devils Tower has been important spiritually for them all. It does not have to be the exclusive property of one tribe in order for the place to be meaningful.

Rather than with a fence, the people will claim some places only with their hearts. We see this phenomenon occur from one end of the continent to the other. The people "belong" to the land in the way that the Navajo, who have always lived within Mount Taylor's majestic view, belong to the mountain. The Navajo never lived *in* the mountains, of course, because such places are too sacred for human habitation. Nonetheless, they know in their hearts that First Man and First Woman created it, along with Blanca Peak, San Francisco Peak, La Plata Mountains, Gobernador Knob, and Huerfano Mountain. These are the symbols that define the boundaries of the Fifth World. It was into this world that the Navajo brought with them all that First Man taught them, such as the names of things and the ways of the *yeis*, the sacred beings "who can perform magic and travel swiftly on sunbeams."

Alert Bay, Cormorant Channel, Marine Park, British Columbia

In the end, the earth should not be taken for granted. For the lesson implicit in many creation stories, in which floods and fires destroy worlds, is that the world of today is not guaranteed to last forever. It is not that the creators do not love their creations, but rather it is that sometimes life becomes poisoned, making its destruction necessary. This is what happened to the Lakota, who endured the destruction of two previous worlds because the Creating Power became displeased with the bad way people behaved. They made the world "bad and ugly," so a new world was needed. After creating a third world, the Creating Power commanded the people to behave like proper human beings by living in peace with each other and with other living things. When the Creating Power was done, after he had given the people the sacred pipe to live by, he said ominously to the people: "Someday there might be a fourth world."

As long as there is wonder and awe, danger and heroism, life and death, there will be people turning the world around them into myths. But the most profound legends will be the ones about the earth and the gratitude people must show to its life-sustaining forces. For what the creators made when they formed the world out of a handful of mud was a paradox. On the one hand, they gave people a gift that is beyond the capacity of all our prayers and ceremonies to repay. Yet the earth is a gift nonetheless.

Canyon de Chelly National Monument, Arizona

On the other hand, despite the proposition that the creators put the people in exactly the right place, it is beyond the ability of anyone to truly own it. "I will die," proclaimed Roman Nose, the great Cheyenne leader, "but only the mountains and rocks are forever." When you look at the Badlands or Canyon de Chelly, or anyplace, you can sense the veracity of Roman Nose's statement. We are reminded of this anytime we look through a family photo album and see departed loved ones enjoying places that remain while the loved ones have vanished. The only thing that will remain are memories, which are really stories. And when stories are about departed loved ones, they are about ancestors, which brings our stories to the brink of legend.

Remembering and retelling legends is a ceremonial act. While reading the legends in these pages, we cannot forget the fact that these were stories that were meant to be told. Read the stories aloud. Read them for other people. For legends only come to life when they find sustenance in the storyteller's voice. What this means to the listeners is that they are bonded by stories in a way that is comparable to kinship ties. This makes sense when you consider that Indian languages are spoken by relatively few people. "You knew your brothers. They spoke your language," as George Linden characterized Dakota philosophy. Linden would go on to say, in light of the fact that no more than 20,000 people speak Dakota, that a "quantitatively restricted language, a language of few speakers, is an intimate language."

What happens then when a little-spoken language is used to tell stories is that it creates an aural environment that is shared by all who can listen and understand. A story "engulfs, surrounds, and envelops us. It unifies and unites according to interior relationships." Consequently, when legends are told, they reinforce a world view that can be expressed only in the words of the people. In a sense, then, a story does not extend beyond the boundaries of the world it describes. We lose some of this intimacy, of course, when legends are translated into more commonly used dialects. Nevertheless, the spirit of these tales is still there, along with the spirit of the places they invoke. With that it is hoped that the reader will feel engulfed and surrounded by a sense of fulfillment at knowing where on earth they belong.

—David Martínez, Ph.D.
American Indian Studies
University of Minnesota, Twin Cities Campus

Sources on p.159.

PHOTOGRAPHING THE NATIVE LANDSCAPE

As I read the remarkable legends of the North American Indian peoples, retold by David Martínez and collected in this book, I began to understand the powerful bond between native peoples and their lands. Profoundly spiritual, American Indians view these lands as divine gifts. They believe they must care for the lands so that they remain forever in the pristine state in which they were received—devoid of monuments, temples, or shrines that would mar their natural beauty and grandeur. In keeping with their belief that spirits imbue all of creation, their legends grew naturally out of their deep respect for the elements and forces of nature as well as for other living creatures that inhabited and continue to inhabit their lands.

As I trekked across the North American continent in search of the visual images these ancient tales evoke, I discovered breathtaking landscapes. When visiting Indian reservations and unspoiled lands in Canada, the United States, and northern Mexico, I could not help but share American Indians' awe for the natural world and admire the centuries of harmony these respectful caretakers have had with these lands. As I traveled, I found that my reading of the legends had begun to influence my perceptions. Gazing at the mountains, ravines, forests, and valleys—even at the moon, clouds, and rain—I began to visualize the mythological events they described.

I particularly remember an experience on a Hopi Indian reservation in the great Southwest. The Hopis have lived for more than a thousand years on four spectacular mesas in northeastern Arizona, among the oldest continuously inhabited communities in the Americas. These dry mesas offer only a few springs, seeps, and washes to their inhabitants—a geological reality that has had a fundamental impact on the people's belief system. It is no wonder that the Hopi believe that when they die, they become benevolent beings, known as kachinas, and take the form of clouds. According to legend, these Cloud People, whose substance is liquid, manifest themselves as rain, thus continuing to help their people long after they have gone. This Hopi belief is a wonderful example of the association of nature and mythic events, between land and legend, which make the extraordinary landscapes included in this book come alive.

While standing on these mesas and looking up at the clouds, I remembered this and imagined the ancestors of today's inhabitants, raining sustenance upon them from above. The internalization of this myth influenced my choice of locations as well as the framing and composition of the photographs themselves—resulting in a special prominence being given to the skies and clouds above these mesas. As with the Hopis, so in every place I visited, I attempted in a subjective and personal way to depict the magic of myths and legends that grew out of these lands. My quest was to visually capture the powerful and timeless link between these ancient peoples, their magnificent lands, and their enduring legends.

—Elan Penn, Ph.D.

Wikaninnish Bay, Pacific Rim National Park, Washington

31

2

LEGENDS & LANDS FROM THE SOUTHWEST

The Southwest, a vast, mostly arid region, stretches from the southern California coast to the Rio Grande in west Texas and from southern Utah and Colorado south into northern Mexico. Its varied and dramatic topography includes the Grand Canyon of Arizona, the Mogollon Mountains of New Mexico, and desert country along the Little Colorado River.

In this harsh terrain with little rainfall, the American Indians of the Southwest developed both nomadic and agrarian lifestyles. Permanent villages, most with Pueblo-style architecture with multiple apartments made from adobe bricks and ladders connecting the different levels, sustained themselves with finely tuned agricultural skills. The Acoma established one of the oldest settlements in New Mexico, and the Pima had a vast system of irrigation canals. Semi-nomadic Indians, such as the Navajo and Apache, often built wickiups and hogans covered in earth for shelter or more permanent homes. These nomads, who relied on hunting and gathering food, sometimes raided Pueblo crops to supplement their diets.

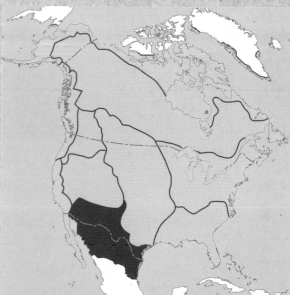

Lands of the American Indians of the Southwest

Many Southwest tribes have been thought to descend from earlier Southwest peoples, such as the Hopi, Zuñi, and the Rio Grande Pueblo peoples from the ancient Anasazi, who enjoyed a sophisticated culture that dates back to about 1500 b.c. The Anasazi grew corn and squash and made baskets which they covered with clay and baked to form fire-proof containers.

PAGE 32: *Canyon de Chelly National Monument, Arizona*

TOP: *Mojave Desert*

The Five Worlds

It begins with a small world surrounded on all sides by a great ocean. The sky is a hard shell with yet no sun or moon. However, the four directions have been set—with white in the east, blue in the south, yellow in the west, and black in the north. Below are insect people who are arguing because adultery has been committed. They begin crawling around the sky, looking for an exit. They are forced out by their bad behavior.

The insect people enter the second world, which looks much like the first world, but is populated by various bluebird people. The bluebird people accept the exiles into their world. But again the insect people commit adultery and are ejected from the second world. Only with the help of Nilch'i, the wind, do the insect people find their way into the third world. There they find the yellow grasshopper people, with whom they immediately commit adultery and get expelled from the third world.

After being forced to flee three previous worlds, the insect people have resolved to be more chastened and refrain from stirring disorder. When they enter the fourth world, they encounter people living in square houses. They are also confronted by Talking God and the other yeis, who perform an elaborate ceremony. They put two ears of corn, one yellow and one white, underneath two buckskins. Nilch'i blows on the corn and they are transformed into First Man and First Woman.

First Man and First Woman have several sets of twins, all the while learning how to hunt, farm, and make beautiful baskets and pots. The twins marry into a group called the Mirage People. To strengthen the bond between men and women, First Woman creates the penis and the clitoris. Coyote then came along and blew some of his whiskers in between the legs of the men and women, thereby causing men and women to cover themselves up in the presence of others.

All went well for eight years. First Man taught the people the names of the four most sacred mountains on the horizon. He also taught them the ways of the holy people, the yeis, who can perform magic and travel swiftly on sunbeams. Unfortunately, trouble broke out among the people.

One day when First Man returned with a deer for dinner, First Woman thanked her vagina. First Man was shocked. First Woman explained that if it were not for woman's vagina, men would not do any work. First Man was outraged. The two began arguing,

Mount Taylor, New Mexico

and their discord grew until First Man decided to leave for the other side of the river, taking all the men with him. First Woman asserted that women did not need men for anything.

The men and women stayed this way for quite a while. In the women's camp there was enough food to get them through winter, while the men hunted successfully for themselves. Occasionally, the women would go down to the river and taunt the men with what they could no longer have, just to make certain that the men still desired them. Eventually, though, the women began suffering due to the lack of food. Some even drowned while attempting to cross the river.

What made matters worse was that men and women still longed for each other. The women tried to satisfy themselves with stones, quills, and even cacti. The men sought satisfaction with mud and deer livers. Finally, after four years of disharmony, Owl warned the men that they could not reproduce themselves, causing them to die off. What made this matter all the more urgent, Owl said, was that the women were in great peril.

First Man sent a messenger for First Woman, asking her to come down to the river. When they met, First Woman admitted that women needed men, and First Man apologized for his behavior. Men and women were at last rejoined.

Before this occurred, though, two young women were taken by a monster, Big Water Creature. Two people and some of the yeis tried to rescue them but failed. So Coyote went out and snatched them from Big Water Creature. He then hid the two women in his coat and brought them to shore.

After all this, the fourth world came to an end. A great flood came in from all four directions. The people asked Squirrel for help, so he planted nuts that became fast-growing trees. The trees, however, did not grow high enough. Weasel then planted seeds, but these trees did not grow high enough either. Then two mysterious men, one old and one young, appeared with a bag of soil gathered from the four most sacred mountains. With a ceremony, they spread the contents on the ground, out of which a great reed grew with an opening on its eastern side. The people went into this as the reed continued growing, keeping the people just above the raging waters. At last, the people made it into the fifth world, the glittering world, where they live today.

The White Dawn of the Hopi

A long time ago there was nothing but water on the earth. Huruing Wuhti lived in the east, in a kiva out in the ocean. Gray and yellow fox skins hung from the kiva's ladder. She had power over rocks, clays, and minerals. To the west lived another Huruing Wuhti, but in a smaller kiva with a turtle-shell rattle hanging from the top of the ladder.

When the Sun rose each morning in the east, he put on the gray fox skin, making the white dawn. As he ascended, the Sun would trade the gray fox skin for the yellow, making the sky brighter. He then left the eastern kiva for the west. As the Sun arrived in the west, he fastened on the turtle-shell rattle. He then entered the western kiva, disappearing into the night. Upon entering the western kiva, the Sun passed underneath the water on his way back to Huruing Wuhti's kiva in the east.

The two Huruing Wuhtis caused the waters to recede, exposing dry land below. The Sun noticed, though, that there were no living beings upon it. The three of them discussed the absence of creatures, after which, they decided to create a little bird. The Huruing Wuhti of the east made a clay wren, covering it with a piece of *möchápu*, native cloth. The two Huruing Wuhtis sang over this and the bird came to life. They then sent the wren in search of other living creatures. The wren returned, saying he found nothing.

Many birds of different kinds were made in the same manner as the first. Songs were sung, and the birds were brought to life. Each bird was taught its own sound, then sent out to different parts of the world.

The Huruing Wuhti of the west proceeded to make various animals, teaching them their respective languages and sending them to the four directions. But it was time to create humans.

First they made a white man and a white woman. Then they made two tablets on which characters were engraved, which they gave to the man and woman. The humans could not understand the tablets, so the Huruing Wuhtis rubbed their palms, enabling them to comprehend the tablets. The humans were then taught their language, after which they went to the Huruing Wuhti's kiva in the east, traveling there on a rainbow. They stayed for four days, at the end of which they were told to find a place to live. The couple traveled around for a long while until they found a fertile field, where they built a small simple adobe house.

"All of this is not yet finished," said the Huruing Wuhti of the west to her eastern sister.

Spider Woman was aware of what the Huruing Wuhti sisters were doing, so she created her own man and woman, teaching them Spanish. She also made burros for them, and they settled down near her home. Spider Woman also made other kinds of people, each with a different language. However, there were times when Spider Woman did not create a man to go with a certain woman and the other way around. Spider Woman instructed the single woman to search for the single man, and see if they would accept each other. The two found each other and, fortunately, accepted each other.

"Where shall we live?" they asked Spider Woman.

"Why, anywhere," asserted Spider Woman.

The man then went to work building a house for them. Before too long, though, they began to quarrel.

"I want to live alone," the woman declared. "I can cook for myself."

"But who'll get wood for you and work the fields?" the man rebutted.

They made up, but it did not last, and they began quarreling again. They went through this several times. Because they could not get along very well, other couples learned quarreling from them. This is why today there are still many arguments between husbands and wives.

Painted Desert, Petrified Forest National Park, Arizona

The Huruing Wuhtis made more people of their own, always in pairs. But wherever Spider Woman's people came into contact with them, there was trouble. People lived a nomadic life at this time, hunting and gathering. Because the people roamed about so much, they would often have quarrels about sharing hunting areas with other people.

Finally, the Huruing Wuhti of the west said to all the people, "You stay here. I will live in the middle of the ocean out west. When you need anything, pray to me out there." The people were truly sorry to see her go. The Huruing Wuhti of the east did the same thing. Hopi who need anything deposit their prayer offerings in their villages. When they say their prayers, they think of the two Huruing Wuhtis who live far away, hoping that they still remember them.

Origin of the Clans

A long time ago, when the Hopi were emerging out of the first world in search of the land of the rising sun, they thought it would be fun to play a name game.

When the first band of people came upon a dead bear, they took it as a sign that they should be called the Bear Clan. Another band came along, saw the same dead bear, but then noticed gopher holes around the carcass. They took this as a sign that they should be called the Gopher Clan. Still another band came along and found a nest of spiders, taking it as an indication that they would now become the Spider Clan. At this point, the Bear Clan was far ahead of the other clans, always traveling with Chief Bahana. In later years, people reflected that the Bear Clan always seemed to be first in many things.

Spider Clan usually trailed behind because they had so many children. One day they came across a friendly spider sitting near her large web. The Spider Clan circled around the web as the friendly spider spoke, saying, "I am Spider Woman, possessed of supernatural power. Since you are named for my people, I will help you in any way I can."

"Thank you, Spider Woman," replied the Spider Clan Chief. "We are traveling in search of the land of the rising sun. Other clans are much farther ahead of us. We wish that we could travel faster, but we have so many children."

"Perhaps I can do something to ease your journey," said Spider Woman.

"What can you do for us?" asked the Chief.

"First, I need something from you," said Spider Woman. "You must go into my secret room where you'll find a large water jug. Wash yourself, saving the dust and skin that rolls off of your bodies; then bring that substance to me."

After traveling such a long way, the Chief was covered in layers of dust. He gave a large ball of dust and skin to Spider Woman. Spider Woman then spread a white, fleecy cloth in front of her. She then placed the dust and skin ball in the center, which she rolled carefully into a white ball.

Spider Woman sang a ceremonial song over it four times. The Spider Clan people looked on expectantly. Spider Woman touched the fleecy ball now and then with her web. She sang four more times. Suddenly, the fleecy, white ball moved back and forth on its own. Out of the fleecy ball emerged a tiny animal with four tiny legs.

Spider Woman called her creation a "burro." The creature was small, and the Spider Clan knew that it needed to grow larger and stronger before it would be of any use to them. Spider Woman took charge of caring for the burro. After four days, the burro was ready to travel with the Spider Clan. The people packed their belongings onto the burro, then set out on their search for the land of the rising sun.

Once the Spider Clan left, Spider Woman decided to create a man who would know about caring for the burro during the people's long journey. Unfortunately, when that man caught up with the Spider Clan, he turned out to be selfish. Instead of helping the people, he ran away one night, taking the burro with him. Although the people were disappointed by the loss of their burro, the Spider Clan continued with their search for the land of the rising sun, carrying their burden on their shoulders like before.

Naturally, the Bear Clan was the first to arrive at the final destination. They set about founding the village. Gradually other clans joined them, making their own villages nearby. From this village the Hopi people grew and prospered.

But the Spider Clan, which arrived last in the land of the rising sun, became the largest and most prosperous of all the clans, because they had so many children in the years to come.

First Mesa Hopi Indian Reservation, Arizona

At the Rainbow's End

Long ago when First Woman was created, she fully matured into a beautiful woman in four days. She found herself with many suitors. First Woman did not love any of them, but she did enjoy the company of the handsome ones. Of them all, she thought the Sun was the most attractive. At the same time, First Woman thought that the Sun would never want to take her as his wife.

One day, to First Woman's surprise, the Sun came up behind her and tickled her neck with a feathery plume. First Woman then felt engulfed by warm sunshine. She had become the Sun's wife. Later, she would bear him a son.

After this occurred, First Woman was resting beneath an overhanging cliff when drops of water fell upon her. Once again, First Woman gave birth to another male child. Her two sons became known as twins, Monster-Slayer and Born-for-Water.

They lived together in Navajo Country, surrounded by the four most sacred mountains, Monument Valley and the Painted Desert. Threatening their idyllic existence, however, was a Great Giant that roamed the country. The Great Giant at first wanted to kill and eat First Woman, but he fell in love with her beauty. But First Woman would have nothing to do with him. The Great Giant became all the more resentful when he noticed the twins' footprints outside of First Woman's hogan.

First Woman knew the Great Giant's intentions, so she dug a hole in the middle of her hogan, in which she hid her twin boys. When the Great Giant came around again, he wanted to kill and eat the twins.

"Where did these children come from?" the Great Giant asked First Woman.

"I have no children," replied First Woman.

"You're not telling the truth. I can see the children's footprints in the dirt around you."

"These are only my hand prints. I am very lonesome for children, so I make these tracks myself."

"Very well," said the Great Giant, "I believe you."

First Woman would always have to watch out for the Great Giant as the twins grew. Once the Great Giant even caught sight of the twins and tried to run them down and capture them, but the boys were too fast.

Because the boys were on the verge of becoming men, the spirit who had made First Woman appeared at the hogan one day with a bow made of cedar.

"It's time that you learned to hunt," First Woman said to her first-born son. "We must make some arrows first, as well as a bow for your brother."

"Mostly, we want to hunt for our father," said the first-born son. "Who is our father, anyway, and where does he live?"

"Your father is the Sun, and he lives very far away in the east."

The twins decided to head east with their newly made bows and arrows in search of their father. They traveled as far as they could, but they did not have any luck in finding him, so they went back home.

"We ventured far to the east," the twins told their mother, "but we could not find our father anywhere. Are you sure that he is there?"

"He must have gone to the south," replied First Woman.

So the twins went south as far as they could, but they did not find their father. Their mother then told them to head west, which they did to no avail. Then they were told to head north, only to find the same disappointment. Meanwhile, First Woman was simply glad that they were out of Great Giant's sight.

"We have traveled four times in search of father," the twins said to their mother, "we cannot find him anywhere."

Navajo Indian Reservation, Arizona

"Now I will tell you the truth," First Woman said. "Your fathers, the Sun and the Water-God, live very far away in the middle of the western ocean. Between here and there are great canyons, whose walls clap together and would crush you.

"Even if you somehow make it through the canyons, there are terrible reeds you must cross. They have long knifelike leaves that will cut you to shreds.

"Then, even if you make it through the reeds, you will never make it across the Grand Canyon. In the end, you will never make it across the water to your fathers' home in the western ocean."

"But we must try," the twins said to their mother.

Knowing that they were going to leave, First Woman taught her sons a song of protection.

> *"We are traveling*
> *In an Invisible Way*
> *To seek our fathers*
> *Sun-God, Water-God."*

With that the twins departed for the western ocean. Singing their protective song in sets of four, the twins traveled for many long days. Along the way, they passed a spider hole. From the little hole they heard a voice say "Sssh!" four times. The twins looked back and saw Spider Woman.

"Do not be afraid of me," Spider Woman said, "I am your grandmother. Come into my lodge."

"We cannot enter because your lodge is too small," said the twins.

"Blow toward the east, south, west, and north," instructed Spider Woman.

The twins did as instructed, then saw the spider hole grow large enough for them to enter. Inside they saw the lodge walls covered with bundles of bones wrapped in spider webs.

"These are the bones of men I have killed," said Spider Woman.

Spider Woman talked with the twins about the perils awaiting them on their journey. She taught them songs and told them what to do about the obstacles they would face.

"I will give each of you a magic Feather-Plume," Spider Woman told the twins. "Hold it before you as you travel; it will carry you safely forward. Be on the lookout, though, for a little man with a red head and a striped back."

Painted Desert, Petrified Forest
National Park, Arizona

The twins thanked their grandmother for her help, then went on their way. Before too long, they ran into the man with the red head and the striped back.

"Do not scorn me because I am small," said the man. "I only wish to help you. Put your hands down on the ground and spit into them four times. Now close your fists, saving the saliva for when you come to the western ocean. There you may wash your hands."

The twins thanked the man for his help and resumed their journey. It was not long before they heard the terrible crashing of canyon walls. The twins sang Spider Woman's songs, holding the Feather-Plumes in front of them. The canyon walls stopped crashing long enough to let the twins through safely.

The twins then came across the field of knifelike reeds. Once again, they sang Spider Woman's songs and held the Feather-Plumes in front of them. The reeds miraculously turned into cattails, which opened a wide path for the twins.

When they reached the Grand Canyon, the twins traveled along the rim until they returned to where they started. They could find no way to cross it. The twins sat down and sang both Spider Woman's songs and their mother's. When they opened their eyes, a beautiful rainbow appeared. The rainbow became a bridge extending across the Grand Canyon and over the Colorado River.

The Mittens, Monument Valley Navajo Tribal Park, Arizona

After the twins crossed over the Rainbow Bridge, they continued west for a long time until at last they came to the shore of the western ocean. The ocean was so vast that the twins stopped and wondered how they would ever reach the Turquoise House of their fathers.

The twins washed the saliva off their hands. They sang and prayed. Once again, the Rainbow Bridge appeared, stretching out across the waters to the Turquoise House. The twins raced across to the Turquoise House, where they found their fathers, the Sun and the Water-God, waiting for them at the end of the Rainbow Bridge.

LEFT: *Totem Pole and Yei Pai Chei, Monument Valley Navajo Tribal Park, Arizona*

Legend of the Night Chant

Long ago, there were three brothers who called themselves Diné, the people. The eldest brother was rich. The second brother was a gambler. And the youngest was a growing boy. They had a sister who did not live far from them with her husband.

The middle brother was in the habit of gambling away his brothers' property. He would always return with tall tales about meeting yeis and seeing wondrous places. His brothers never believed him and called him "the dreamer."

One day, the eldest and youngest brothers decided to go hunting but did not want their middle brother to come along. Without telling the dreamer, the other two asked their brother-in-law to come along on the hunting trip. It would be four days before the dreamer realized what had happened. The dreamer went looking for the hunting party, figuring that he would help bring back the game and maybe be rewarded with a pelt or two.

The dreamer traveled far before the sun went down behind the hills in the distance. Nearby was a canyon with steep cliffs, out of which wafted the sound of voices. The dreamer peered over the edge. Within the canyon were countless crows flying back and forth. Through the cawing of crows the dreamer heard a voice call.

"They say! They say! They say!"
Then there was a reply of "Yes, yes, what's the matter now?"
"Two people were killed today," said the first voice.
"Who were they?" asked the second.
"Ana-hail-ihi was killed at sunrise and Igak-izhi was killed at dusk. Both by the earth people. They went in search of meat, and hunters shot arrows into them. We are sorry. They were told to be careful, but they did not listen. It's too late to help them now. Let's continue with the chant."

Betatakin, Navajo National Monument, Arizona

The dreamer was frightened, all the more so since it was getting dark. But the dreamer could not pry himself from the cliff edge. The sound of singing echoed throughout the canyon. The yeis were singing! The dreamer also saw a distant fire below, by which he could see the faint outlines of figures dancing, keeping time with their rattles. The dance went on until dawn, at which time the dancers departed. Finally, the dreamer continued his search for his brothers.

When the dreamer at last located the hunting camp, he was anxious to tell his brothers what he had seen the night before. His two brothers and brother-in-law responded with ridicule. The dreamer was frustrated but continued to tell them all what had happened. Most important, he told them about the yeis's concern for the two people killed. That got their attention.

"Well, it wasn't any of us," asserted the brother-in-law. "We haven't killed any people. So far, all we've done is shoot at a crow and a magpie."

"I think that's what the yeis were talking about," said the dreamer. "The yeis must have been disguised as birds while they searched for meat."

Just then they saw four mountain sheep. All of them grabbed their bows and arrows. Each one was ready for the kill, but when the dreamer had the lead sheep in his sights, he could not release the arrow. This happened three more times as the sheep worked their way down the canyon wall. When the dreamer looked at the sheep again, they had transformed themselves into four yeis, who were now approaching the dreamer.

The leader quickly came up to the dreamer and dropped his *balil* (a rectangular, four-piece folding wand) over him. The yei then let loose a peculiar cry and the other three yeis appeared beside him. All of them wore masks.

Monument Valley Navajo Tribal Park, Arizona and Utah

"Where did you come from?" the dreamer asked.

"From Kinni-nikai," the leader said.

"Where are you going?"

"To Taegyil, to conduct another chant four days from now. Will you come with us?"

"I could never travel that far in four days."

The yeis told the dreamer not to worry, and asked him to disrobe. The leader then breathed upon the dreamer, who was now dressed like a yei. They then stepped toward the east in unison, turning themselves into mountain sheep.

All of this happened somehow without the other three being aware of it happening. All they found were the dreamer's old belongings and human footprints that suddenly became mountain sheep tracks.

On the fourth day, the four mountain sheep reached a hogan, in which several holy people awaited them. When the dreamer entered, the holy people waiting began to complain of an earthly, human odor. So the leader took the dreamer outside and washed him with yucca suds.

Inside the hogan stood four large jewel posts, upon which the yeis hung their masks. The eastern post was made of white shell, the southern one of turquoise, the western one of abalone, and the northern one of jet. Two jewel pipes lay beside a yei seated to the west side of the hogan. Filling both pipes with tobacco, the yei lit them and passed one to his right and the other to his left. Each took his turn smoking in the hogan. The last to take their turns were two large owls sitting on either side of the entrance facing east. As this was going on, people kept coming to the site from all four directions. One of them was Water Sprinkler, who came in with a flash of lightning and thunder. Some of the yeis came in with sandpaintings painted on white deerskins. They set these in the middle of the hogan one at a time as needed during the chant.

The last day of the chant was well attended. The dreamer all along paid careful attention to all of the details. He took in all of the songs, prayers, sandpaintings, and dances. When the chant was completed the dreamer had learned the *Kieje Hatal*, the Night Chant.

Spider Rock

During the Fourth World, monsters roamed the earth, killing people and eating them. Because Spider Woman loved the people, she gave power to the twin sons of First Woman, Monster-Slayer, and Born-for-Water, so that they could find their fathers, the Sun and the Water-God. They would show the twin boys how to rid the land of these awful creatures.

Spider Woman lived in Canyon de Chelly, on top of Spider Rock. Aside from helping Monster-Slayer and Born-for-Water, Spider Woman was also known for teaching women how to weave using a loom. She was known as well for punishing children who did not know how to behave themselves, coming down from the top of Spider Rock to snatch them away. Parents told their children that the top of Spider Rock was white from the bones of the children she had eaten.

One day a young man was hunting in Dead Man's Canyon, a branch of Canyon de Chelly. Suddenly, he saw an enemy tribesman, who began chasing him through the canyon. The young man looked from side to side in hope of finding a place to hide.

Directly in front of him was a great rocky spire standing in the middle of the canyon floor. He knew that it was too steep for him to climb, and he was nearly exhausted. Just then he noticed a silken cord hanging down from the top of the spire.

The young man grabbed hold of the cord and tied it around his waist. The cord then began hauling him upward and out of reach of the enemy below. Soon the young man was safe as he went higher while watching the enemy give up the chase and walk away.

When the young man made it to the top, he untied himself and rested. Afterward he discovered that there were eagle's eggs for him to eat and the night's dew to drink. As he replenished himself, the young man was surprised to see Spider Woman. She told him how she had seen him and his predicament. She showed him how she made her strong web cord and how she anchored one end to a rocky point. Then she showed him how she lowered the other end so that she could pull him to safety.

The young man was eternally grateful for what Spider Woman had done for him. Spider Woman told him that it was safe for him to go, so she lowered him back down to the canyon floor. The young man ran home as fast as he could, to tell his people how he was saved by Spider Woman.

Spider Rock, Canyon de Chelly
National Monument, Arizona

The Four Flutes

Long ago, the Zuñis wanted new music and dances for their ceremonies, but they did not know how to go about creating such things.

The Chief and his counselors went to the Elder Priests of the Bow to ask for their help. "Grandfathers," the Chief said, "we are tired of the same old music and dances. Can you please show us how to make new music and dances for the people?"

After much deliberation, the Elder Priests decided to ask the Wise Ones to visit the God of Dew. The next day, four Wise Ones set out on their mission.

Their journey took them up a steep trail into the Sacred Mountain. From somewhere above, the four Wise Ones were pleased to hear music. After climbing the trail higher, they discovered that the music came from the Cave of the Rainbow. Vapors floated about the entrance, a sign that within this cave was Paíyatuma.

The four Wise Ones asked permission to enter the cave, and suddenly the music stopped. After a moment of silence, Paíyatuma offered a warm welcome to the visitors. He then said, "Our musicians will rest now while we learn why you have come here."

"Our Elders, the Priests of the Bow, asked us to come. We wish for you to show us the secret of making new music and dances. As gifts, our Elders have prepared these prayersticks and special plume-offerings for you and your people."

"Sit with me now," said Paíyatuma. "You will now see and hear."

Many musicians appeared before them wearing beautifully decorated long shirts. Their faces were painted with the signs of the gods. Each held a lengthy tapered flute. In the center of the group was a large drum, beside which stood the drummer.

Paíyatuma stood and spread corn pollen at the feet of his visitors. With crossed arms he strode the length of the cave, turning and walking back again. Seven beautiful young women, tall and slender, followed him. The young women were dressed much like the musicians. They held hollow cottonwood shafts from which bubbled delicate wisps of cloud as they blew into them.

"These are not corn maidens," Paíyatuma informed the Wise Ones. "They are our dancers, the sisters from the House of Stars."

Paíyatuma put a flute to his lips and joined the circle of dancers. The drummer beat a thunderous rhythm, shaking the cave walls, indicating that the dance would begin.

Beautiful music from the flutes seemed to sing and sigh like the gentle blowing of the winds. Bubbles of vapor arose from the sisters' reeds. Butterflies flew about the cave, keeping with the beat like the other dancers. All the colors of the rainbow mysteriously lighted the cave from floor to ceiling. The four Wise Ones felt as if they were dreaming.

At the end of the performance, they thanked Paíyatuma for his help. Paíyatuma then came up to the four and breathed on each one. He also summoned four of the musicians, asking them to give each of the four Wise Ones a flute.

Ojo Caliente, Zuñi Indian Reservation, New Mexico

"Now go back to your Elders," Paíyatuma said. "Tell them what you have seen and heard here. Give them these flutes. And may your people learn to sing like the birds."

The four Wise Ones bowed deeply with gratitude. Finally, after thanking Paíyatuma for the wonderful gifts he had bestowed upon them, they left for their village, going back down the trail that brought them there.

Upon their return, the four Wise Ones presented the Elders with the four flutes. The Wise Ones described and demonstrated what they had learned at the Cave of the Rainbow. The Chief and his counselors were very happy with this new knowledge. From then on the people would enjoy the new music and dances.

*Zuñi Indian Reservation,
New Mexico*

Culture Hero

Piankettacholla was born long ago to a woman who had never known a man. Nevertheless, Piankettacholla was born because when his mother put some pebbles in her belt she was soon afterwards big with child. The people wanted to kill the child when they could not find out who the father was. The mother, though, was able to protect her child, and he grew up to be very handsome, "like Jesus Christ."

Piankettacholla taught the people to dance, to make clothes, and to plant corn, beans, and melons, which he made from different colors of stones.

Piankettacholla could fly. He fastened to his breech cloth an eagle's tail, and to his arms above the elbows, wild turkey wings. He could get within a few feet of the stars, which are actually birds.

The star-birds have very green legs and bright breasts like the hummingbird. They also have a bill like an eagle and very dark eyes. When the stars twinkle is when the star-birds are flying slowly. When they fly much faster than normal is when they appear as shooting stars. When you cannot see the stars is when the birds have turned around.

Piankettacholla, however, was unable to learn how the star-birds lived; nor could he get near enough to the sun and moon to find out more about them.

Sometimes Piankettacholla would go down into the earth. During summer, he brought up ice and snow, while during the winter he brought back green leaves. In fact, Piankettacholla, which means "mountain point green-blue," got his name from being able to make the mountains green by making it rain.

Taos Pueblo, Taos, New Mexico

One time a great flood of hot water came and drowned all the people, except for Piankettacholla, who saved himself by hiding in a big pile of cottonwood bark. He looked down and saw where it was green, and there he made the waters go down. He came out of the bark pile, took some foam from the waters, and made people. From different colors of stones he made seeds, which the people planted.

Piankettacholla then warned the people about the coming of the whites, the Spanish, Mexicans, and Americans. He said that the Indian people would become fewer and fewer until the day when all would be white.

Piankettacholla still lives in a lake to the north of Taos. One time a noise, like the beating of a drum, was heard in the lake. His tracks have been seen around there as well. He is very old but he does not die.

Turquoise Boy Races the Deer Boys

Turquoise Boy was living with his grandmother at the Edge-of-the-Grass. He was a good hunter. About this his grandmother said, "You are going farther and farther away. You may not go beyond to the east."

One day Turquoise Boy went over the mountain and met a bunch of deer. They said to him, "Turquoise Boy, what are you doing here? You should be back with your grandmother at the Edge-of-the-Grass."

"I know that I am far from home," said Turquoise Boy.

"What pretty turquoise you have," the deer said. "Let's run a race around the world!"

"This is what my grandmother was afraid of. Now I must tell her what the Deer Boys have said to me."

When Turquoise Boy arrived back home at the Edge-of-the-Grass, he said, "Grandmother, you told me not to go beyond to the east, but I went anyway. When I got there, the Deer boys said that they liked my turquoise and challenged me to a race around the world."

"This is what I feared, grandson," said the grandmother. "Well, now, you must go and see your Grandmother Gopher. She has power and may help you."

Turquoise Boy went to Grandmother Gopher's home and said, "Grandmother Gopher, I have come to ask for your help. The Deer Boys have challenged me to a race around the world for my turquoise."

"Yes, grandson, I will help you," said Grandmother Gopher.

"Now I have to work on the road." By that she meant that she was already familiar with the route that the race would take.

Turquoise Boy and the Deer Boys met at the divide down at Blue Lake. The Deer Boys brought a pile of mantas and some other goods. Grandmother Gopher brought a bowl of turquoise. She then gave Turquoise Boy some medicine.

The race started with the Deer Boys quickly out in front. As Turquoise Boy came up behind, he spat out some of the medicine. Many gopher holes appeared in the road ahead so the Deer Boys had trouble running.

Turquoise Boy took the lead as they approached Coyote Ears House. However, the Deer Boys passed ahead again as they turned and headed south. Turquoise Boy shouted, "Kwialalumu, make yourselves strong!" He then gained on the Deer Boys at Mountain of White Earth. The Deer Boys slowed down as they went into the mountain.

But the Deer Boys were still in the lead. So Turquoise Boy spat out more medicine and berry bushes appeared before the Deer Boys. "Eat with us," said the berry bushes to the Deer Boys, and the Deer Boys stopped to eat. Turquoise Boy took the lead.

But once again it did not take long for the Deer Boys to take back the lead. So Turquoise Boy spat out more medicine and fruit appeared, which the Deer Boys stopped to eat.

Turquoise Boy saw Taos Peak in the distance. He then approached Fog House. People watching the race tried to see who was in the lead. Some thought the Deer Boys were ahead, while others were certain that it was Turquoise Boy. Out of the fog the Deer Boys came limping with cracked hooves.

Turquoise Boy was declared the winner. The people gave Turquoise Boy the mantas, wrapped leggings, and the whole pile of goods that the Deer Boys had wagered.

Grandmother Gopher gave her bowl of turquoise to all. "So you may help the world," she said. "That the world may live longer!"

Turquoise Boy and his grandmother lived happily after this. As they were leaving for home, Turquoise Boy said to the people, "All who want to be good hunters may come to the Edge-of-the-Grass and ask me."

Taos Pueblo, Taos, New Mexico

Enchanted Mesa

Long ago the Acoma people lived on *Ka-tse-Ma*, which is called Enchanted Mesa today. The mountains around this country were in harmony with the needs of the people, yielding plentiful crops in the fields below. The people were strong.

One day it was decided that the old people would stay atop the Enchanted Mesa with the children while all the others worked the fields below. The rains had been good recently, making for a splendid growing season. At one point, the old people told their young ones working that they had more than enough food for the winter.

Unfortunately, because of their desire to get as much from the land as possible, they began to overwork the earth.

As the people worked the fields for more than they could give, a rainstorm moved into the valley. The young people ignored the storm and kept on working. But the rain kept coming, and soon it was pouring like it had never done before. The fields were becoming flooded. Finally, the people decided that they had better head back to their homes atop the Enchanted Mesa.

But the rains had come down so hard that the only path back to the top had eroded away. When it seemed that the rain would never stop, the people began to panic and weep for their loved ones left on top of the mesa.

The rain lasted for many days. With the path and the fields washed away, all the people in the valley could do was wait. However, because of the despair that several of them felt for their family members above them, some just became sick and died.

Enchanted Mesa, Acoma Indian Reservation, New Mexico

Migration of the Parrot Clan

Long ago, when all the clans were searching for their current homes, the Parrot Clan people were second only to the Bear Clan in importance. When the Parrot Clan began its migration, they started from the south, a direction regarded as fertile and fruitful. Nonetheless, there were very few Parrot Clan people. Because of this, an old man and woman were fearful that their people would die out before finishing their migration northward. So the old couple went looking for medicine that would enable them to grow and become stronger.

As the old couple searched for medicine, they met a stranger who took them to his home. They were greeted by a beautiful woman, who said to the old man and woman, "I heard your prayers for the power of fertility. So I sent my messenger to bring you here. Now I will give you this blessing."

The beautiful woman showed the old man and woman to a nest that was in the corner of her home. In the nest were eggs of various colors. "Kneel down and put your right hand on the eggs," the beautiful woman said to the old woman. "Pray now for the blessing you want." Once the old woman had done as she was told, it was the old man's turn to do the same thing.

After they both finished their prayers, they sensed the movement of life in the eggs.

"Good," said the beautiful woman. "Take your hands off of the eggs. You may know now that these are parrot eggs and that you are now Kyáshwunga, Parrot Clan people. You will have the power of fertility, and your people will multiply. In the ages to come, other clans will ask for your power to increase. You must not deny them this power, for you are Yumuteaota, Mother People. Remember me and what I say, for I am the one who looks after all of the bird people."

Wupatki National Monument, Arizona

The old man and woman returned happily to the rest of their clan. They continued with their migration, watching the people multiply along the way.

First they went northward through Pusivi, "Big Cave," near Nogales, where they turned west and came upon the Pacific Ocean. They then headed east and stopped at Kyashva, "Parrot Spring," in the Grand Canyon, followed by a stop in Walnut Canyon, which was settled by the Chosnyam, the Blue Jay People.

From there they went northwest, passing through small ruins on the plains, and followed up the east side of the Great Divide through Canada toward the Back Door. But their journey did not end there. On their way back down west, they stopped at several places, including Túwi'i near Santo Domingo Pueblo, Wénima, Pavi'ovi, and Chosóvi, near the Tonto ruins. They also stopped at Walnut Canyon and Wupatki, "Tall House," near Flagstaff.

Finally, they reached their home in Shongopovi and Oraibi.

Creation of the Sacred Mountains

First Man and First Woman formed six sacred mountains from the soil that First Man had gathered from the mountains in the Third World, which he kept in his medicine bag. They placed Sis na'jin, Blanca Peak, in the East. Tso dzil, Mount Taylor, was set in the South. Dook'oslid, San Francisco Peak, was set in the West, and Debe'ntsa, La Plata Mountains, was placed in the North. They also made Choli'i'i, Gobernador Knob, and Dzil na'odili, Huerfano Mountain, around which people would have to travel.

First Man called the four Holy Boys to him. He told White Bead Boy to enter Blanca Peak. He then told Turquoise Boy to go into Mount Taylor. Next, he told Abalone Shell Boy to enter San Francisco Peak. Lastly, First Man asked Jet Boy to enter La Plata Mountains.

The mountains to the East and South, Blanca Peak and Mount Taylor, were dissatisfied. They wanted to trade Holy Boys. To show their dissatisfaction, they would tremble horribly. The other two mountains, to the contrary, were perfectly content. First Man and First Woman called other Holy Beings to them.

They asked the Beautiful Mixed Stones Boy and Girl to enter Gobernador Knob. Then they put Pollen Boy and Grasshopper Girl into Huerfano Mountain. Once this was done, they told Rock Crystal Girl to go into Blanca Peak, followed by White Corn Girl going into Mount Taylor. Yellow Corn Girl was then placed into San Francisco Peak, with Darkness Girl coming last, entering La Plata Mountains.

First Man and First Woman now proceeded with fastening the mountains to their respective places in Navajo Country. Blanca Peak was fastened with a bolt of white lightning. They covered the mountain with a blanket of daylight, decorating it with white shells, white lightning, black clouds, and male rain. The white-shell basket was placed on the summit, in which were laid two pigeon eggs. Pigeons would be the mountain's feather. Last, the bear was asked to guard the doorway of the White Bead Boy in the East.

San Francisco Peak, New Mexico

First Man and First Woman then fastened Mount Taylor with a stone knife. They covered this mountain with a blue cloud blanket, decorating it with turquoise, white corn, dark mists, and female rain. A turquoise basket was set on the highest peak, in which were laid two bluebird eggs. Bluebirds were this mountain's feather. Lastly, the big snake was asked to guard the doorway of the Turquoise Boy in the South.

San Francisco Peak was fastened with a sunbeam. They covered this mountain with a yellow cloud, decorating it with haliotis shell, yellow corn, black clouds, and male rain. Many animals would live in this mountain. An abalone shell basket was placed on the summit, in which were laid two yellow warbler eggs. Yellow warblers would be this mountain's feather. The Black Wind was asked to guard the doorway of the Abalone Shell Boy of the West.

La Plata Mountains was fastened with a rainbow. First Man and First Woman covered this mountain with a blanket of darkness, decorating it with bash'zhini, obsidian, black vapors, and various plants and animals. An obsidian basket was placed on the highest peak, in which were laid two blackbird eggs. Blackbirds would be this mountain's feather. Finally, the lightning was asked to guard the doorway of Jet Boy in the North.

Gobernador Knob and Huerfano Mountain were also fastened and decorated by First Man and First Woman, though their summits did not have any baskets.

Nevertheless, all of the six mountains were given prayers and chants, which when performed, are called "Dressing the Mountains." All the corner posts of a hogan also have their prayers and chants, as do the stars and the earth. It is their custom to keep the sky and the earth, as well as the day and the night beautiful. The belief is that if this is done, life among the people will be good.

Migration of the Badger Clan

Long ago, the Bear Clan led a number of other clans southward to the land's end. After going as far as they could, they began heading back. Somewhere along the way, some of the people decided to turn west, while the rest ventured east.

While traveling through a warm country, a little girl became terribly ill. No one was able to cure her. So the oldest member of the group decided to seek some power or medicine that would help her. The old man began following an unusual track, which led him to a stranger.

"I am Honani, the Badger," said the stranger. "How can I help you?"

Upon learning of the little girl's illness, Honani dug up an herb and gave it to the old man to take home with him. The old man was then to boil the herb and give the broth to the girl. Honani also showed the old man other herbs that would be useful to the people for other illnesses. "You should always remember to pray," Honani said. "Medicine should always be accompanied by prayer and good thoughts."

The old man returned to the people with his medicine gifts. Following Honani's instructions, the little girl was soon cured of her illness. "In recognition for what this spirit being has done for us," the old man declared, "we should now be known as Honani's people, the Badger Clan."

The Badger Clan continued its migration northward, stopping at Palátkwapi, Red House. They saw evidence of other clans stopping before them, so they became anxious to move on. As they persevered, they stopped to replenish their food supply at Honinyaha, Badger Earth Dam. After this, they went on until they reached the Rio Grande, following it north until they found somewhere suitable for planting and harvesting their two crops. They next stopped near

Petroglyphs, Mesa Verde National Park, Colorado

Chi-yá-wi-pa, which today is called San Felipe. Onward they continued on their northward journey until they came into mountains so cold that it was impossible to dwell there. Instead, they turned back toward Toko'navi, which is called Navajo Mountain today. They headed westward toward the Pacific.

The Badger Clan stayed next to the western ocean for four days, planting their shrine. At the end of this time, they went east toward the Atlantic, where they planted another shrine and watched the sun come up four times. They began heading back west, a little north of the trail they used traveling east. They slowed down when they reached the mountains of southern Colorado.

The Badger Clan continued to increase its numbers during all these years of migration. So much so that the clan divided up into Brown, Gray, and Black Badger Clans. The latter was the oldest and held the position of leadership. However, the old man who founded the original Badger Clan had become very old and weak over the years.

Mesa Verde National Park, Colorado

"We have completed our migrations to the four ends of the earth," the old man told his people. "Clearly, it is time for us to settle down and build a village. We will wait here for a sign of our final destination."

The leaders of the Brown and Gray Badger Clans did not like the idea much, but they obeyed. They built their houses, storerooms, and kivas inside of a beautiful canyon, which had a huge cave in a cliff. After settling down, the Butterfly Clan joined the village, and the village grew into large numbers. Discontent arose among the people. Their quarreling continued until the rains and snow stopped coming. Soon the corn began to wither and the game disappeared. The people began to suffer.

The old man called all the people together and said, "Clearly it is time for us to leave. Your quarreling has brought great misfortune. We must now go our separate ways."

The old man looked sad as he spoke.

"I am too old and feeble to join any of you. I must ask you to leave me here. However, in four years come back to this place. Look for me in important places—the kivas, the shrines, the springs. If I am to blame for any of your misfortune, you will not find any sign of my having been here. But, if my heart has been true, you'll find a sign, and you'll know what to do. Go now and remember what I have told you."

All of the Badger Clan abandoned the village, separated, and continued their migration. Four years later, the Badger Clan leaders returned as they were asked. What they found was a clear sign that the old man's heart had been true. During his hour of death, the old man went down to a spring just below the village and turned into a spruce tree. What was a dry spring when the people were quarreling was now gushing with water, beside which was a four-year-old spruce.

The people decided to honor the old man's memory. Each year, during the Niman Kacina ceremonies, they send a messenger to plant prayer feathers at the spruce. The prayers ask the old man to participate in their ceremonies. The messenger then brings back a piece of the spruce tree as a token of the old man's assent. Salavi ("Spruce") was his name, and the village he founded was called Salapa, which today is called Mesa Verde.

Cliff Palace, Mesa Verde National Park, Colorado

3

LEGENDS & LANDS FROM THE GREAT PLAINS

The Great Plains stretches from southern Manitoba, Saskatchewan, and Alberta in the north to central Texas in the south, and from the Mississippi River west to the Rocky Mountains. These predominantly flat grasslands are marked by a predictable sameness and include vast expanses of grazing lands for the North American buffalo (bison). In the northern Great Plains are the Bighorn forests of Wyoming and Montana; the Badlands of South Dakota, rugged semi-arid lands with soil erosion, deep gullies, and deep-rooted plants because of short, heavy showers that sweep away surface soil and small plants; and many northern plateaus with spectacular formations.

Lands of the American Indians of the Great Plains

Great Plains American Indians developed a subsistence pattern of living after contact with the Spanish and other Europeans, who brought horses. Tribes who once dwelled in villages and farming communities became nomadic hunters of game, especially the buffalo. Other tribes also migrated to the Great Plains to take advantage of this new lifestyle and more rewarding hunting. Great Plains tribes are made up of bands of related families who lived apart but reunited in summer for ceremonies and hunting. Many lived in tipis, while semi-nomadic tribes built more permanent dwellings, such as grass huts. Great Plains Indians include the Crow, Lakota, Mandan, and Cheyenne, among others.

Old Man Coyote Makes the World

How water came to be, nobody knows. Where Old Man Coyote came from, nobody knows. But there he was at the beginning.

Old Man Coyote said, "It is bad that I am alone. I should have someone to talk to. It is bad that there is only water and nothing else." As Old Man Coyote walked around wondering what to do, he spotted two ducks. He called them "younger brothers" and asked one of them to dive into the water in search of something besides water.

One of the ducks dove in immediately and was gone for a very long time. Old Man Coyote feared that the duck had perished. At long last, though, the duck reappeared with a small bit of mud on its bill. Old Man Coyote took the mud from the duck's bill and blew on it in the palm of his hand. Instantly the lump of mud began to grow. "This is wonderful, elder brother!" the ducks said. "We are pleased."

With the ducks at his side, Old Man Coyote molded his creation into a beautiful place with grasses, plants, trees, and all sorts of food. He also added hills and mountains, as well as rivers, ponds, and streams, "so that wherever we go," Old Man Coyote said, "we can have cool, fresh water to drink."

At this point, they all gazed at the world with awe, but then wondered what, if anything, could be missing. "Companions," declared Old Man Coyote. "We are alone. It's boring."

So Old Man Coyote fashioned men out of mud and he was pleased. But then the ducks asked for companions, so Old Man Coyote made many ducks. However, all the companions were of

PAGE 74: *Badlands National Park, South Dakota*

RIGHT: *Bighorn National Forest, Wyoming*

one gender, so Old Man Coyote made women and female ducks, and they began to multiply. Everyone was happy.

After this, Old Man Coyote wandered around his creation. While doing so, he ran into coyote, his younger brother. It was coyote, then, who pointed out to Old Man Coyote that there ought to be more than just ducks in the world. Old Man Coyote was surprised by this oversight, so he began naming animals, which immediately began to appear. He named the buffalo, deer, antelope, and bear.

After creating these creatures, the bear spoke to Old Man Coyote. "Why did you make me? There's nothing to do. We're all bored." Old Man Coyote knew that the bear was right, there had to be something more. Then it came to him.

Old Man Coyote took one of the bear's claws and made wings. From a caterpillar's hair he made feet. From a bit of buffalo sinew he made a beak. From leaves he made a tail. From all these things he made a prairie chicken. Old Man Coyote then told the prairie chicken how to dance. At once, the prairie chicken danced. All the animals watched and began dancing as well.

Bear was still unsatisfied. He wanted his own dance, so Old Man Coyote gave all the animals their own dance. Bear was still unsatisfied. There was nothing to dance to, so Old Man Coyote created a grouse and a drum. Now there was drumming and singing. All the animals danced. But bear was still unsatisfied. Bear wanted to be the only animal who danced.

"Why should you be the only one?" Old Man Coyote asked.

"Because I am big and important!" cried bear.

"Listen to him," Old Man Coyote said indignantly. "Be polite to the one who made you."

"Ho! You didn't make me," asserted bear, "I made myself."

Old Man Coyote had heard enough. "You're not fit to live among us," declared Old Man Coyote. "You will stay in a den by yourself and eat decayed, rotten things. In the winter you will sleep, because the less we see of you, the better." So it was.

Old Man Coyote was pleased with the way things were, but coyote, his younger brother, told him that something was still missing. Old Man Coyote wondered what he could have possibly forgotten.

"The people are poor," coyote said. "They should have tipis and fire."

"You're quite right," Old Man Coyote said, and with that the people had tipis and fire.

"Elder brother, they should also have weapons for hunting, so they won't starve." Once again, Old Man Coyote agreed, so he gave the people spears, bows, and arrows. But when Old Man Coyote wanted to give the animals weapons, too, coyote warned him not to.

"Why shouldn't the animals have bows and arrows as well?" Old Man Coyote asked.

"Don't you see?" coyote said, "The animals are swift. They already have big claws, teeth, and powerful horns. The people are slow. Their teeth and nails are not very strong. The people wouldn't survive if the animals also had weapons."

Convinced by coyote's argument, Old Man Coyote refrained from giving the animals weapons. But coyote was not satisfied with the way things were. Coyote wanted there to be more than one language, for the reason that people could not fight a war with other people if they all spoke the same language.

"What good are wars?" Old Man Coyote asked.

Coyote explained that wars were good for the honors and prestige they can bring men. Most of all, proving yourself in war is a great way of wooing women. "You gaze at the good-looking young girls," coyote continued. "You look at the young women whose husbands have no war honors. They look back at you.

Little Bighorn Battlefield National Monument, Crow Indian Reservation, Montana.

On June 25, 1876, at Little Bighorn, Sioux and Cheyenne warriors led by Chief Crazy Horse (Ta-Sunko-Witko) and Chief Sitting Bull soundly defeated General Custer and his Seventh Cavalry of the United States Army that had attacked an American Indian encampment.

You go on the warpath. You steal the enemy's horses. You steal his women and maidens. You count coups, do brave deeds. You are rich. You have gifts to give away. They sing songs honoring you. You have many loves. And by and by, you become a chief."

Old Man Coyote was very impressed by this portrayal of war. So Old Man Coyote created the different tribes, each speaking a different language, and each becoming the rival of the other. With that, there was war and all that coyote said would come of war.

The last thing that Old Man Coyote did was talk with coyote about the virtues of taking back a wife who has been stolen from you.

Crow Indian Reservation, Montana

"Why would anyone do such a thing?" coyote asked.

"Three times my wife has been abducted, and three times I have taken her back," Old Man Coyote said. "Whenever I ask her to do something, she remembers that she was stolen. She is eager to please. She fulfills my every desire. Under the blanket she's a hot one—she has learned things. This is the best wife, the best kind of loving."

"Don't you care about being mocked by others?" coyote asked.

"What do I care if anyone laughs when, under the buffalo robe, I'm laughing for my own reasons? Let me tell you, there's nothing more satisfying than a wife who's been stolen once or twice."

With Old Man Coyote's advice, there was mutual wife stealing during the old days. That's why Crow men will take back their wives, even after they have been divorced. In one way or another, everything that exists or happens goes back to Old Man Coyote.

How the Lakota Came To Be

A long time ago, when the world was still freshly made, Unktehi the water monster fought with the people and caused a great flood. Perhaps Wakan Tanka, the Great Spirit, was angry with the people. Maybe he let Unktehi win because he thought he could create a better kind of people.

Whatever the reason, the waters got higher and higher. Eventually, everything became flooded except a certain hill in the distance. People rushed to climb to the top, but to no avail, as the floodwaters swept over the pinnacle.

The blood of those killed began to pool. The pool, however, turned into pipestone, becoming the pipestone quarry of today, from which the people make their pipes. The red pipe bowl is made from the blood of ancestors. The pipestem is the backbone of those dead ones. The smoke rising is their breath. This is why the pipe, the *chanunpa*, is so sacred.

Unktehi was also turned into stone. Maybe Tunkashila, the Grandfather Spirit, punished her for causing the flood. Unktehi's bones are in the Badlands today. Her back forms a long, high ridge, with her vertebrae sticking out as a great row of red and yellow rocks.

Only a single girl survived the flood. When the waters engulfed the hill where all the people fled, a great spotted eagle, Wanblee Galeshka, flew down and allowed the girl to grab hold of its claws. The spotted eagle then alighted atop a tall tree that stands on the highest stone pinnacle in the Black Hills. This was Wanblee Galeshka's home. It was also the only place that the flood did not consume.

The spotted eagle kept the girl with him and made her his wife. As his wife, the girl bore Wanblee Galeshka twins, a boy and a girl. The spotted eagle's wife was happy and said, "Now we will have people again. *Washtay*, it is good."

When the floodwaters finally receded, Wanblee Galeshka helped his wife and children down from his lofty home to the earth below. He told them, "Be a nation, become a great nation—the Lakota Oyate." The boy and girl grew up into a handsome young man and a beautiful young woman. As the only people on earth, they married and had children. The Lakota nation was born.

Badlands National Park, South Dakota

First Creator and Lone Man

In the beginning, the surface of the earth was nothing but water and there was darkness all about. First Creator and Lone Man were traveling across the waters when they ran into a duck floating by itself. They asked the duck to show them how it survived. The duck then dove into the deep waters and returned with a ball of sand. First Creator and Lone Man assumed upon seeing this that the sand must be good for other creatures as well.

"Let us make land out of this substance, and living creatures," they said. First Creator and Lone Man then divided their work between them, which they marked with the Missouri River. First Creator took the southern half, while Lone Man took the northern.

First Creator made broad valleys, hills, coulees with timber, mountain streams, and springs. He also made the buffalo elk, black-tailed and white-tailed antelopes, mountain sheep, and a bevy of other creatures that would be useful to humankind.

Lone Man, for his part, made a mostly level country with lakes, small streams, and rivers set far apart. The animals he made lived in the water, like the beaver, otter, and muskrat. He also made moose and cattle, which came in different colors, not to mention having long horns and tails.

After surveying all they had done, First Creator told Lone Man that his creation did not meet with his approval. For the land that Lone Man made was too level and would not afford people a very good living. First Creator argued that he had taken much better care of the needs of people. Lone Man, of course, protested against First Creator's appraisal of his land, asserting that it was just as good for people as any other. They realized, however, that what was done could not be undone. In light of this, they agreed that people would use the things that First Creator made until the supply was exhausted, after which the people would then use the things that Lone Man had made. Once this was settled, they each blessed their creations, then parted.

Lone Man, however, wished to live among the people, whom he saw multiplying on the earth. Before going to them, he picked a young woman who would be his mother, who became pregnant with him when she ate a particular ear of corn. In due time, the young woman had a baby boy.

The child grew up like any other Mandan. When he became a man, though, he had an unusual desire to spread goodness. If ever a quarrel arose between people, he would pacify them. He loved children, and they would follow him around wherever he went. Every morning he purified himself with incense.

One day, a group of men were getting ready to sail down a river where they would reach an island. There they would gather *ma-ta-ba-ho*. Their boat, however, could carry only twelve men and no more, otherwise they would have bad luck. But the man—who was really Lone Man—came along and insisted that he go with the crew. The men in the boat protested, but Lone Man was persistent. When the men realized that they were not going to get rid of Lone Man, they relented and allowed him to board their vessel.

Unsurprisingly, it was not long into the journey that evil spirits began assaulting the voyagers. Lone Man, however, would rebuke the evil spirits every time they surfaced from the water, and tell them not to be evil spirits any longer. When they passed along a patch of willows, the trees turned into men who called out to men to come ashore and wrestle with them.

Only Lone Man was willing to accept the challenge, easily defeating all of his opponents by throwing them into the river. As they got closer to the ocean, a whirlpool appeared, into which the men began throwing offerings, hoping to pacify the wild waters. Lone Man grabbed all the offerings, saying that they were for him. The men murmured against Lone Man, accusing him of bringing them bad luck. But Lone Man rebuked the whirlpool, saying, "Do you not know that I am the one who created you? Now I command you to be still." And the whirlpool desisted, and the boat passed through unharmed.

Bighorn River, Crow Indian Reservation, Montana

Tongue River Reservoir, Montana

Eventually, they reached the island, which was ruled by a chief named Ma-na-ge. The chief did not care for the visitors and wanted to kill them. Ma-na-ge thought he would do this by inviting the visitors to a great feast, at which he would make them eat beyond capacity, then do away with them. Lone Man foresaw this and told the men to eat very little from the dish as it was passed around and give the bulk to him.

The men obeyed his instructions, and when the overflowing dish reached Lone Man, he poured the contents into a bulrush, which then passed into the fourth stratum of the earth. "Well," Lone Man said to his host, "I had always heard that this village was always generous with visitors. But if this is all that you have, I would hardly call it a feast." The chief was astounded that people could consume so much without becoming sick.

Undaunted, the chief invited the men to smoke with him. Just as with the feast, the chief thought to make the men smoke a huge quantity until they were ill, then do away with them. Lone Man, once again, foresaw this and told the men not to take in too much of the tobacco. When the enormous pipe came to Lone Man, he inhaled with a great heave and smoked out the entire contents of the pipe. The chief was beginning to suspect something peculiar about these men, especially Lone Man, whose identity was yet unknown.

At last it was time to collect the ma-ta-ba-ho. The chief told the visitors that they may take home as much ma-ta-ba-ho as their bags could carry. They lined up and had their bags filled in turn. When it was Lone Man's turn, he produced a rather small bag. The chief laughed at how tiny the bag was that Lone Man held out. But when they began putting in the ma-ta-ba-ho, the bag refused to fill to the top.

Finally, the chief shouted, "You think that I don't know who you are, Lone Man?"

"Perhaps I am Lone Man," Lone Man said as he walked away.

"After you return home, we will come to visit your village on the fourth night," Ma-na-ge threatened the crew as they left the shore of the island.

Upon reaching home, Lone Man instructed his people on how to perform the ceremonies that were devoted to him. They were to clear a round space in the middle of the village, build a barricade around it, then use four young cottonwoods as a hoop. The center would hold a cedar painted with red earth, to which the people would burn incense and make offerings.

Lone Man said, "This cedar is my body that I leave with you as protection from all harm, and this barricade will protect you against any dangerous waters. Ma-na-ge will come, and the sign of his arrival will be a heavy fog that will last for four days and nights. Do not fear; the fog is nothing but water. And the water will rise no higher than the first hoop next to the ground. When it can get no higher, it will subside."

Lone Man then told his people that now that they were fully instructed in his ways, he would leave them. He then promised to return to them someday, but they had to remember him. With that, he departed southward. Ma-na-ge then came in the form of water, and he tried in every way to destroy the village, but when he failed to rise higher than the first hoop, he subsided.

Wakinyan Tanka, the Great Thunderbird

Wakinyan Tanka, the Great Thunderbird, lives in his tipi, which is atop a high mountain in the Black Hills.

The Wakinyan hates all that is dirty. He loves what is clean and pure. His voice is the great thunderclap, and the smaller rolling thunders that follow his booming shouts are the cries of his children. Four paths lead to the mountain on which the Wakinyan dwell. A Butterfly guards the entrance to the East. A Bear guards the West, a Deer the North, and a Beaver the South.

There are four large old Thunderbirds. The Great Wakinyan of the West is the most prominent among them. He is draped in clouds. His body has no form, but he has giant, four-jointed wings. He has no feet, but enormous claws. He has no head, but a huge, sharp beak with rows of big, pointed teeth. His color is black.

The second Wakinyan of the North is red. The third Thunderbird of the East is yellow. The fourth Thunderbird of the South is white. From time to time a holy man will catch a glimpse of a Wakinyan in his dreams, but never more than a part of it. No one has ever seen a Thunderbird in whole.

The Great Wakinyan's tipi stands beside the tallest cedar tree. Inside the Wakinyan's tipi is a nest made from dry bones. In the nest is a giant egg from which the young Thunderbirds are hatched. The Thunderbirds move about in a contrary, counter-clockwise, manner. If you dream of a Wakinyan, you must become a heyoka, a clown. The *heyoka* is an upside-down, forward-backward man. The Thunderbirds, though, are the guardians of truth, who ultimately like to help the people.

The Thunderbirds were there when the Unktehi grew angry with the people and flooded their land. When this happened, the Great Wakinyan said, "What is to be done? These humans respect us; they pray to us. Although they are small and helpless, Grandfather put them on earth for a reason. We must save them from Unktehi!"

A great battle ensued between the Thunderbirds and Unktehi. It lasted many years, making the earth tremble and the waters burst into mighty torrents. As they fought claw-to-claw, Unktehi began to win. The Thunderbirds knew that they could not fight Unktehi on the ground much longer. So all the Thunderbirds gathered in the sky, then at the Great Wakinyan's signal, they let loose a barrage of thunder and lightning.

The forests were set ablaze. The waters boiled and dried up. The earth glowed with heat. The consequence for Unktehi was that of burning up and dying, leaving only her bones behind, which you can see in the rocks of the Badlands. And the few humans that survived, climbed down from their refuge on top of a high rock and praised the Thunderbirds for saving them. In time, the earth was repopulated and all was well.

Badlands National Park, South Dakota

The Mysterious Butte

A long time ago, a young man was out hunting and came across a steep hill. On the east side of the hill was a sudden drop from a precipitous incline. The young man then noticed an opening below him at the base of the hill. It looked small at first, but upon closer inspection the young man discovered that it was large enough for a horse to pass through. When the young man peered in, he was shocked to see animal figures carved into the walls.

The young man went in a little farther and found an array of pipes, bracelets, and other ornaments on the ground. He then discovered another cavern farther in, where it was so dark that he could not see his hand before his face. The young man decided to go back to camp and tell what he saw here.

The chief listened to the young man's story. He then selected four of the bravest men in the village to go back with the young man to see if he was telling the truth.

Upon returning to the cave's entrance, the young man was reluctant to go back in because the animal figures on the wall had somehow changed from before. The other four men went right in and found the place to be as the young man described it; they even found the much darker cavern toward the back. But they did not stop there. They went into the dark cavern, feeling their way along the walls. They came to another entrance through which they could only walk sideways. Then they came to another that forced them to crawl on their hands and knees.

The men were surprised to be drawn by a very sweet odor. They continued crawling forward until they came across a hole in the ground. The sweet odor was coming from there. The four brave

Badlands National Park,
South Dakota

men stopped their pursuit and held council. They decided to return to camp and report what they had learned of this unusual place.

As they reached the outside entrance to the cave, one of the men spotted an attractive bracelet and said that he was going to take this home with him. He wanted it as a token of their adventure.

The other three tried to dissuade him from doing that. "You are in the abode of a Great Spirit. An accident may happen to you for taking something that does not belong to you."

The one man was unconvinced. "You're like a bunch of old women," he said as he tried the bracelet on his wrist.

All four men made it back to camp and told their story. The one with the bracelet showed everyone his token as proof of their tale.

Later on, after everyone had forgotten about the cave, the four men were out setting wolf traps. They raised one end of a heavy log and placed a stick underneath it to keep it propped up. About four paces from the log they placed a large piece of deer meat. They then covered the space between the trap and the bait with poles and willows. At the spot where the stick stood, they dug a hole large enough to hold a full-grown wolf. The idea was to lure the wolf under the trap when he tried unsuccessfully to get at the meat.

While working another trap, the man with the bracelet caught his souvenir on a log, causing the log to fall on his hand. He called his friends for help. They rushed to his aid and pulled the log off him. When they pulled the log away, though, they found that the man's wrist had been broken.

"Now you've been punished," they said. "You've been punished for taking that bracelet from the mysterious butte."

After this accident occurred, another young man went out to visit the mysterious butte. When he looked into the cave, he saw on the wall a figure of a woman holding a pole in her hand. With it she was holding up a large amount of meat that had been laid across another pole. It was broken in two from the weight of so much meat. Surrounding the figure of the woman were buffalo footprints.

Soon afterwards, a great herd of buffalo passed near the village, and many were killed. The women were very busy cutting up and drying the meat. This was the most meat they had seen in quite a long time. When one of the women was hanging up some meat to dry on a pole, it broke in two. So she had to use a second pole, just like in the engraving the young man had recently seen in the cave.

Because of these events, the people began visiting the mysterious butte regularly for signs of what they should do. The butte was a kind of oracle, and the people told its story for generations.

American buffalo (bison),
Madison River, Yellowstone
National Park, Wyoming

Origin of the Buffalo

Long ago, some Cheyenne hunters lived at the head of a rushing stream that eventually emptied into a large cave. Because the people needed food, the chief called a council meeting.

"We should explore the large cave at the end of the stream," he told those assembled. Then he asked, "How many of you are willing to go on this dangerous venture? I know that some of you are quite brave."

At first, no one said a word. Then one young man decided to be the first to speak up, saying, "I will go and sacrifice myself for our people." It seemed that he would be the only one.

The next day, this brave young man went to the mouth of the cave. When he arrived, he was surprised to see two other young men ready to join him. Into the cave they went, but the darkness was all encompassing, and it took them a while to adjust their eyes.

Farther and farther they crept through the dark cavern. Just when they thought there would be no end to this thing, they found a door! The first brave man knocked, but there was no answer. He knocked again, only harder.

"What do you want, my brave ones?" The three men were surprised to hear a grandmotherly voice speak to them in their language.

"Grandmother," the first brave said, "we are in search of food for the people."

"Are you hungry now?" she asked.

"We are very hungry, Grandmother."

The old woman then opened the door to let in the three brave but starving young men. She led them to a window, through which she pointed at something she wanted them to see. "Look there!" she told them.

They saw a beautiful wide prairie with a great herd of buffalo grazing contentedly. The grandmother brought the young men a stone platter topped with buffalo meat. She invited them to eat as much as they wished, which they did until they felt their stomachs bursting. To their astonishment, the stone platter remained filled with buffalo meat.

"I want you to take this stone platter of buffalo meat back to your people," the grandmother instructed the three young men. "Tell them that soon I will send them live buffalo."

"Thank you, thank you, thank you, kind Grandmother!" the three braves said together before departing for camp.

When the three men returned home with the stone platter of buffalo meat, the people rejoiced at the wonderful new food. Everyone had their fill, feeling content, relieved, and grateful.

When the people awoke the next morning, herds of buffalo had mysteriously appeared, surrounding the whole village. What a wonderful day! The people were truly thankful for what the grandmother did for them. They thanked the Sky Spirits for their good fortune.

American buffalo (bison), Custer State Park, South Dakota

How the Buffalo Hunt Began

There was a time when the buffalo ate the people. Because the people were in peril, they held a council to decide what to do. Magpie and hawk were there because they did not eat people and were on their side in this matter. At the end of the council, they all decided that they would challenge the buffalo to a race, with the winner having the right to hunt the loser.

The buffalo accepted the challenge. They chose a long course around Devils Tower. The people were concerned about the distance, so they tried to get medicine to ward off fatigue. The buffalo, however, were quite confident that they would win, especially with Neika, "Swift Head," running for them.

All the birds and animals painted themselves for the race. Since this time they have been colored the same way. Even the turtle put red paint around his eyes. The magpie painted his head, shoulders, and tail white. Once they were ready, they lined up for the start of the race.

The race began. Instead of singing, many animals made loud noises in order to make themselves run faster. All the small birds, turtles, rabbits, coyotes, wolves, flies, ants, bugs, and snakes were soon left far behind. Neika was in the lead with magpie, hawk, and the people in hot pursuit. All the rest strung along behind.

For the whole race so far, Neika led the pack. Magpie and hawk, however, knew they would win. They were just biding their time until they got close to the finish line. When the finish appeared after Neika circled the whole of Devils Tower, she was certain that victory was hers. Just then, magpie and hawk whooshed past her and won the race on behalf of the people.

At the end of the race, those who finished saw that many animals had run themselves to death. They had fallen along the way, turning the ground red with their blood.

Devils Tower National Monument, Wyoming

Because the people had now won the right to hunt the buffalo, the adult buffaloes told their children to hide from the people. Before they left, the buffalo took human meat with them for the last time, placing it in front of their chests, beneath the throat. Because of this, the people never eat this part of the buffalo, saying that it is human flesh.

From that day onward, the Cheyenne hunted the buffalo. Since all the friendly animals and birds were on the people's side, they are not hunted and eaten by the people. However, they will wear the birds' beautiful feathers as ornaments.

Eagle War Feathers

Once there was a time when the Cheyenne did not know how to use the eagle for their war ornaments. In light of this, one man climbed a high mountain and went for five days without food, crying for a vision. He prayed that some powerful being would visit him and teach him something that his people could use, something great.

Finally, a voice said to him, "Try to be brave, no matter what comes, even if it might kill you. If you remember my words, you will return something great to your people, helping them."

Then there was silence. From out of the silence, seven eagles came down. They wanted to fly away with the man. He remembered what he was told, though, and he tried to be brave. He kept his eyes closed, however, and continued to pray. As he lay there, the seven eagles surrounded him.

He heard one say, "Look at me." The man opened his eyes. "I am powerful and I have wonderfully strong feathers. I am greater than all other animals and birds in the world."

The eagle showed the man his wings and tail, spreading his feathers as widely as possible. Then he showed the man how to use eagle feathers, making the war headdress and other ornaments.

"Your people must use only eagle feathers. They will be of great help to them in war, bringing them many victories," the eagle said.

All seven eagles then shook many of their feathers loose, letting them fall to the ground for the man to gather. The man was very grateful to the eagles and very carefully collected all the feathers.

The man then took his gift home with him.

After returning to camp, the man showed his people what the eagle had shown him. From that day forward, the man became a great warrior and chief, having led many victorious war parties. He became so successful that his people named him Chief Eagle Feather, as he led them with dignity and pride.

Pink Ridge, Northern Cheyenne Indian Reservation, Montana

Coyote, Iktome, and the Rock

Coyote was walking one day with his friend Iktome, the Spider. Along the way stood Iya, the Rock. This was not just any rock, it was quite special. It was covered with green moss and emanated power.

"Why, this is a nice-looking rock," Coyote said to Iktome. Coyote then took off the nice blanket he was wearing and draped it over the rock. "Here, Iya, take this blanket from me as a gift to keep you warm."

"Wow, a giveaway!" exclaimed Iktome. "You're certainly in a giving mood today."

"It's nothing. I'm always giving things away. Iya looks nice in my blanket."

"His blanket now," said Iktome.

The two friends continued with their walk. As they strolled, though, it became increasingly cooler. It began to rain; then the rain turned to hail. Coyote and Iktome sought shelter in a cave, which was freezing and dank. As they waited for the weather to turn, Coyote regretted having given away his blanket. Iktome only looked on, wrapped warmly in a buffalo robe. Coyote asked his friend if he would go back to the Rock and retrieve his blanket before he froze to death. Iktome did as his friend asked. When he reached the Rock, Iktome asked for the blanket.

"No," the Rock said, "I like it. What is given is given."

Iktome returned empty-handed, telling Coyote what the Rock said. "That good-for-nothing rock!" Coyote said angrily. "Did he pay for the blanket? It's mine! I'll go get it myself."

"Be careful of the Rock's power," Iktome warned his friend.

When Coyote reached the Rock, he snapped at him, saying, "Hey, rock! What do you need a blanket for? Give me my blanket back."

"No," the Rock said, "what is given is given."

"Ahhh! Don't you even care that I'm freezing to death?" cried Coyote. Coyote then grabbed the blanket off of the Rock and put it on his shoulders. "That's the end of that."

"By no means is it the end of that," said the Rock ominously.

By the time Coyote caught up with Iktome at the cave, the sun was out again, making everything nice and warm. The two friends sunned themselves, ate pemmican, fry bread, *wojapi*, and berry soup. After finishing their meal, they took out their pipes and had a smoke.

"What's that noise?" Iktome asked all of a sudden.

"I don't hear anything," said Coyote.

"It's a distant rumbling noise."

"Oh, yes. I hear it now."

"It's getting louder. It's very strange if it's thunder."

"It seems to be coming this way," said Coyote. "I wonder what it could be."

Just then they saw the rock heading for them.

"Run for it!" shouted Iktome, and they both ran. It was obvious that the rock wanted to kill them.

"Let's swim across the river," said Iktome, "I'm sure the rock will only sink." So they swam as fast as they could. To their dis-

may, the rock made it across the water like he was made of wood.

"Let's run through the forest," said Coyote, "I'm sure the rock will get stuck between the trees."

So they ran through the forest. To their dismay again, the rock barreled through the dense forest, relentless in his pursuit of the two friends. Upon coming out of the forest, Coyote and Iktome found themselves on the prairie.

When Iktome spotted a mouse hole, he decided that this was not really his quarrel, so he rolled himself into a tiny ball and disappeared into the mouse's home.

All Coyote could do was keep on running. But he was running out of breath. At that point, the rock overtook Coyote and flattened him like a leaf. The rock then took back the blanket and left Coyote for the vultures.

Just then a white rancher came along and saw the flattened Coyote lying on the prairie. "What a nice rug," he said, and took poor Coyote home with him. What the rancher did not know is that Coyote is able to return himself to life again. However, it took Coyote quite a long time to puff himself back into his normal shape. So one morning the rancher's wife wound up telling her husband, "I just saw your blanket running away."

Bighorn National Forest,
Wyoming

Remaking the World

There was once a world before this world. Unfortunately, the people there did not know how to behave properly. The Creating Power was unhappy with the way things turned out. "I will make a new world," he said to himself. The Creating Power then placed his pipe on a rack that was made in the sacred manner. He took four dry buffalo chips and placed three of them under three sticks, saving the fourth for lighting the pipe.

"I will sing three songs," the Creating Power said, "which will bring a heavy rain. Then I will sing a fourth song, stamping four times on the earth. This will cause the earth to crack wide open. Water will come out of the cracks and cover the land."

The Creating Power sang the first song and it started to rain. It began pouring when he sang the second song. When he sang the third song, the rain-swollen rivers overflowed their beds. Finally, he sang the fourth song and stomped on the earth four times. The earth split open in many places like a shattered gourd. Water sprang furiously from the cracks and covered all the land.

The Creating Power floated on his pipe and huge pipe bag. He went this way and that on the waves for a long time. At last the rain stopped, by which time all the animals had drowned. Only the crow survived.

But the crow had nowhere to land, so it had to keep aloft, flying until it was very tired. "Tunkashila, Grandfather," said the crow to the Creating Power, "I must soon rest." Three more times the crow asked for someplace to land.

"It's time to unwrap the pipe and open the pipe bag," announced the Creating Power. The wrapping and the pipe bag contained all kinds of animals and birds, from which he selected four that were known for their ability to stay underwater for long stretches of time.

Prairie dogs, Custer State Park, South Dakota

The first animal chosen was the loon. He then told the loon to dive into the water and bring back a lump of mud. So the loon did as it was told, but was unable to bring back anything. "I could not reach the bottom, and I almost died," said the loon. "The water is too deep."

The second animal chosen was the otter. The otter then dove into the watery depths, and stayed longer than the loon underneath the waves. But it, too, was unable to come back with the lump of mud.

The third animal chosen was the beaver. Like the loon and otter before it, the beaver went into the water with a mighty thrust. So far it had stayed the longest underneath the vast ocean. But it also came back with nothing.

At last, it was the turtle's turn to dive into the sea. "It is up to you to bring back the lump of mud," the Creating Power said to the turtle.

The gentle turtle then slid off the Creating Power's hand and into the water. By far it was gone the longest, so long that the crow overhead—still waiting for someplace to land—was certain that it was dead. Just then the turtle popped up.

"I got to the bottom," said the turtle. "I brought back the mud."

The Creating Power took the lump of mud from turtle and began to sing. He kept on singing while he worked the mud in his hands, forming it into a dry piece of land. Finally the land was big enough for crow to come down and rest. The crow was quite happy.

The Creating Power took two long eagle wing feathers from his bag and waved them over the land, commanding them to spread to the far horizon. "Water without earth is not good," said the Creating Power, "but land without water is also not good." Feeling pity for the earth, the Creating Power wept over his creation, with his tears becoming the lakes, streams, and oceans. "Now it is good."

Working the earth again, the Creating Power made men and women. He used red earth and white earth, yellow earth and black, making many different people. The human shapes came alive when the Creating Power stomped on the earth. The Creating Power gave them all understanding and speech, and told them which tribe they belonged to.

The Creating Power said to them: "The first world I made was bad; the creatures on it were bad. So I burned it up. The second world I made was also bad, so I drowned it. This is the third world I have made. Look! I have created a rainbow as a sign to you that there will be no more great floods. Whenever you see a rainbow, you will remember my promise."

The people looked at the beautiful rainbow as the Creating Power continued admonishing them, saying: "Now, if you have learned how to behave like human beings, living in peace with each other and all living beings, then all will be well. However, if you make this world bad and ugly, then I will destroy it like the others. It is up to you."

The Creating Power gave the people a pipe. "Live by it," he said. He then named this land the Turtle Continent in honor of the turtle who brought back the lump of mud. "Someday there might be a fourth world," the Creating Power thought. At last, he rested.

Stockade Lake, Custer State Park, South Dakota

Chief Roman Nose Loses His Medicine

The Lakota and the Cheyenne have been allies for a very long time. Many times have they fought shoulder to shoulder. They fought the white soldiers on the Bozeman Trail and on the Rosebud River. They also fought together at the Battle of the Little Bighorn, where Custer was defeated.

A long time ago, the Cheyenne had a famous warrior chief, whom the whites called Roman Nose. He had the fierce, proud face of a hawk, and he always rode into battle with a long war-bonnet trailing behind him. He had many eagle feathers for the many great deeds he had accomplished throughout his heroic life.

Roman Nose possessed powerful medicine, which he kept in the form of a stone he had tied in his hair on the back of his head. Before going into battle, he sprinkled gopher dust on his war shirt and painted his horse with hailstone patterns. These things protected him from the white man's bullets, even those fired by enemy tribes. Roman Nose could, however, be killed by a lance, knife, or tomahawk. But nobody ever got the best of Roman Nose in a hand-to-hand fight.

Roman Nose, in order to keep his medicine strong, had to refrain from using anything made of metal while he ate. He had to use horn or wooden spoons and eat from wooden or earthenware bowls. His meat had to be cooked in a buffalo pouch or in a clay pot.

One day, Roman Nose got word of a battle raging between white soldiers and Cheyenne warriors. The fight had been going back and forth all day. When Roman Nose was asked for his help in the fight, he gathered his warriors together. Before joining the battle, Roman Nose and the others had a hasty meal, during which Roman Nose forgot about the restrictions regarding his medicine.

The white soldiers had made a fort on a sandspit island in the middle of a river. They were shooting from behind, and they had a new type of rifle that could shoot faster and farther than the Cheyenne's bows and arrows and old muzzle-loaders.

The Cheyenne flung themselves against the soldiers in wave after wave, but crossing the river was difficult and treacherous in spots, making the attack nearly impossible. Consequently, many warriors were gunned down.

Roman Nose prepared for the fight by putting on his finest clothes, war shirt, and leggings. He painted his best horse with hailstone designs, and he tied the sacred stone into his hair. Just then an old warrior walked up to Roman Nose and said, "You have eaten from an iron kettle with a metal spoon and a steel knife. Your medicine is powerless. You must not fight today. Purify yourself for four days so that your medicine will be good again."

Little Bighorn Battlefield
National Monument, Montana

"But the fight is today," responded Roman Nose, "not in four days. I must lead my warriors. I will die, but only the mountains and rocks are forever."

Roman Nose continued preparing for battle. After he put on his warbonnet, he sang his death song, then he charged into the fight with his warriors beside him. As soon as he got to the riverbank overlooking the sandspit a bullet hit him in the chest. Roman Nose fell from his horse. Cheyenne warriors quickly retrieved their fallen chief's body and took him to safety. Roman Nose was dead.

All through the night the Cheyenne sang mourning songs in honor of Roman Nose. He had died as he had lived. He had shown that sometimes it is better to die like a great chief than to live to see old age.

4

LEGENDS & LANDS FROM THE NORTHEAST

The Northeast region stretches from the Nova Scotia and New Brunswick south along the Atlantic coast to the Tidewater basin of Virginia and North Carolina and west to the Great Lakes and Mississippi River. The landscape has fertile valleys, rivers, lakes, mountains, flatlands, swamps, marshes, and ocean coastline. The customs and lifestyles of the American Indians of the Northeast are largely defined by geography.

The Mahican and Montauk lived in Nova Scotia, New England, and Long Island; and the Mohawk, Oneida, and Tobbaco in New York and Ontario. The Penobscot, Passamaquoddy, Maliseet, and Micmac were in the Maritime Provinces and Maine. Also in the Northeast were the Onondaga, Seneca, Cayuga, and Tuscarora. Tribes sharing common languages, like the Algonquian- or Iroquoian-speaking, shared cultures.

Many Northeast Indians were semi-nomadic, depending on the availability of food. The Northeast was once heavily forested, so trees supplied the

Lands of the American Indians of the Northeast

primary materials for shelter, tools, and fuel. Forest animals and plants provided food, and many American Indians also fished and farmed. Most villages as well as cultivated fields were located near lakes and rivers. Iroquoian-speaking tribes lived in communal dwellings, and Algonquian-speaking tribes tended to live in smaller structures, such as wigwams, reserving larger structures for communal purposes and ceremonial gatherings. Both the Algonquians and the Iroquois formed their own confederacies and appear to have inherited common traditions.

MOHAWK

ONONDAGA

SENECA

CAYUGA

ONEIDA

TUSCARORA

The Origin of the Iroquois Confederacy

Long ago in the great past, there were no people on the earth. All of it was covered by deep water. Birds, flying, filled the air, and many huge monsters possessed the waters.

One day, the birds saw a beautiful woman falling from the sky. Immediately, the huge ducks held a council. "How can we prevent her from falling into the water?" they asked.

After some discussion, they decided to spread out their wings and thus break the force of her fall. Each duck spread out its wings until they touched the wings of other ducks. So the beautiful woman reached them safely.

Then the monsters of the deep held a council to decide how they could protect the beautiful being from the terror of the waters. One after another, the monsters decided that they were not able to protect her, that only Giant Tortoise was big enough to bear her weight. He volunteered, and she was gently placed upon his back. Giant Tortoise magically increased in size and soon became a large island.

After a time, the Celestial Woman gave birth to twin boys. One was the Spirit of Good. He made all the good things on the earth and caused the corn, the fruits, and the tobacco to grow.

The other twin was the Spirit of Evil. He created the weeds and also the worms and the bugs and all the other creatures that do evil to the good animals and birds.

All the time, Giant Tortoise continued to stretch himself. And so the world became larger and larger. Sometimes Giant Tortoise moved himself in such a way as to make the earth quake.

After many years had passed, the Sky-Holder, Ta-rhu-hia-wah-ku, decided to create some people. He wanted them to surpass all

PAGE 108: *Lac Lamarre, Quebec*

RIGHT: *La Mauricie National Park, Quebec*

Mohawk, Onondaga, Seneca, Cayuga, Oneida, and Tuscarora **III**

others in beauty, strength, and bravery. So from the bosom of the island where they had been living on moles, the Sky-Holder brought forth six pairs of people.

The first pair were left near a river, now called the Mohawk. So they are called the Mohawk Indians. The second pair were told to move their home beside a large stone. Their descendants have been called the Oneidas. Many of them lived on the south side of Oneida Lake and others in the valleys of Oneida Creek. A third pair were left on a high hill and have always been called the Onondagas.

The fourth pair became the parents of the Cayugas, and the fifth pair the parents of the Senecas. Both were placed in what is now known as the State of New York. But the Tuscaroras were taken up the Roanoke River into what is now known as North Carolina. There the Sky-Holder made his home while he taught these people and their descendants many useful arts and crafts.

The Tuscaroras claim that Sky-Holder's presence with them made them superior to other Iroquois nations. But each of the other five will tell you, "Ours was the favored tribe with whom Sky-Holder made his home while he was on earth."

The Onondagas say, "We have the council fire. That means that we are the chosen people."

As the years passed, the numerous Iroquois families became scattered over the states, and live in what is now Pennsylvania, upstate New York, the Midwest, and southeastern Canada. Some lived in areas where bear was their principal game. So these people were called the Bear Clan. Others lived where beavers were plentiful. So they were called the Beaver Clan. For similar reasons the Deer, Wolf, Snipe, and Tortoise clans received their names.

La Mauricie National Park, Quebec

The First People and the First Corn

Long ago, Klos-kur-beh, the Great Teacher, lived in the land where no people lived. One day at noon a young man came to him and called him "Mother's brother."

Standing before Klos-kur-beh, he said, "I was born of the foam of the waters. The wind blew, and the waves quickened into foam. The sun shone on the foam and warmed it. And the warmth made life, and the life was I. See—I am young and swift, and I have come to abide with you and to help in all that you do."

Again on a day at noon, a maiden came, stood before the two, and called them "my children." "My children, I have come to abide with you and have brought with me love. I will give it to you. If you will love me and grant my wish, all the world will love me, even the very beasts. Strength is mine, and I give it to whosoever may get me. Comfort is also mine, for though I am young, my strength shall be felt over all the earth. I was born of the beautiful plant of the earth. For the dew fell on the leaf, and the sun warmed the dew, and the warmth was life, and that life is I."

Then Klos-kur-beh lifted up his hands toward the sun and praised the Great Spirit. Afterward, the young man and the maiden became man and wife, and she became the first mother. Klos-kur-beh taught their children and did great works for them. When his works were finished, he went away to live in the Northland until it should be time for him to come again.

The people increased until they were numerous.

When a famine came among them, the first mother grew more and more sorrowful. Every day at noon she left her husband's lodge and stayed away from him until the shadows were long. Her husband, who dearly loved her, was sad because of her sorrow. One day he followed her trail as far as the ford of the river, and there he waited for her to return.

When she came, she sang as she began to ford the river, and as long as her feet were in the water, she seemed glad. The man saw something that trailed behind her right foot, like a long green blade. When she came out of the water, she stooped and cast off the blade. Then she appeared sorrowful.

The husband followed her home as the sun was setting, and he bade her come out to look at the beautiful sun. While they stood side by side, there came seven little children.

They stood in front of the couple, looked into the woman's face, and spoke: "We are hungry, and the night will soon be here. Where is the food?"

Tears ran down the woman's face as she said, "Be quiet, little ones. In seven moons you shall be filled and shall hunger no more."

Her husband reached out, wiped away her tears, and asked, "My wife, what can I do to make you happy?"

"Nothing else," she said. "Nothing else will make me happy."

Then the husband went away to the Northland to ask Klos-kur-beh for counsel. With the rising of the seventh sun, he returned and said, "O wife, Klos-kur-beh has told me to do what you asked."

The woman was pleased and said: "I want you to slay me. When you have slain me, let two men take hold of my hair and draw my body all the way around a field. When they have come to the middle of it, let them bury my bones. Then they must come away. When seven months have passed, let them go again to the field and gather all that they find. Tell them to eat it. It is my flesh. You must save a part of it to put in the ground again. My bones you cannot eat, but you may burn them. The smoke will bring peace to you and your children."

The next day, when the sun was rising, the man slew his wife. Following her orders, two men drew her body over an open field

Adirondacks, New York

until her flesh was torn away. In the middle of the field, they buried her bones.

When seven moons had passed and the husband came again to that place, he saw it filled with beautiful tall plants. He tasted the fruit of the plant and found it sweet. He called it *Skar-mu-nal*—"corn." And on the place where his wife's bones were buried, he saw a plant with broad leaves, bitter to the taste. He called it *Utar-mur-wa-yeh*—"tobacco."

Then the people were glad in their hearts, and they came to the harvest. But when the fruits were all gathered, the man did not

Catskills, New York

know how to divide them. So he sent to the great teacher, Klos-kur-beh, for counsel.

When Klos-kur-beh came and saw the great harvest, he said: "Now have the first words of the first mother come to pass, for she said that she was born of the leaf of the beautiful plant. She said also that her power should be felt over the whole world and that all men should love her.

"And now that she has gone into this substance, take care that the second seed of the first mother be always with you, for it is her flesh. Her bones have also been given for your good. Burn them, and the smoke will bring freshness to the mind. And since these things came from the goodness of a woman's heart, see that you hold her always in memory. Remember when you eat. Remember when the smoke of her bones rises before you. And because you are all brothers, divide among you her flesh and her bones. Let all share alike, for so will the love of the first mother have been fulfilled."

Glooscap Fights the Water Monster

Glooscap yet lives, somewhere at the southern edge of the world. He never grows old, and he lasts as long as this world lasts. Sometimes Glooscap gets tired of running the world, ruling the animals, regulating nature, and instructing people on how to live.

Then he tells us: "I'm tired of it. Good-bye, I'm going to make myself die now." He paddles off in his magic white canoe and disappears in misty clouds. But he always comes back. He cannot abandon the people forever, and they cannot live without him.

Glooscap is a spirit, a medicine man, a sorcerer. He can make men and women smile. He can do anything.

Glooscap made all the animals, creating them to be peaceful and useful to humans.

When he formed the first squirrel, it was as big as a whale. "What would you do if I let you loose on the world?" Glooscap asked, and the squirrel attacked a big tree, chewing it to pieces in no time. "You're too destructive for your size," said Glooscap, and remade him small.

The first beaver also was as big as a whale, and it built a dam that flooded the country from horizon to horizon. Glooscap said, "You'll drown all the people if I let you loose like this." He tapped the beaver on the back, and it shrank to its present size.

The first moose was so tall that it reached to the sky and looked altogether different from the way it looks now. It trampled everything in its path—forests, mountains, everything. "You'll ruin everything," Glooscap said. "You'll step on people and kill them." Glooscap tapped the moose on the back to make it small, but the moose refused to become smaller. So Glooscap killed it and recreated it in a different size and with a different look. In this way Glooscap made everything as it should be.

Glooscap had also created a village and taught the people there everything they needed to know. They were happy hunting and fishing. Men and women were happy making love. Children were happy playing. Parents cherished their children, and children respected their parents. All was well as Glooscap made it.

The village had one spring, the only source of water far and wide, that always flowed with pure, clear, cold water. But one day the spring ran dry; only a little bit of slimy ooze issued from it. It stayed dry even in the fall when the rains came, and in the spring when the snows melted. The people wondered, "What shall we do? We can't live without water."

The wise men and elders held a council and decided to send a man north to the source of the spring to see why it had run dry.

This man walked a long time until at last he came to a village. The people there were not like humans; they had webbed hands and feet. Here the brook widened out. There was some water in it, not much, but a little, though it was slimy, yellowish, and stinking. The man was thirsty from his walk and asked to be given a little water, even if it was bad.

"We can't give you any water," said the people with the webbed hands and feet, "unless our great chief permits it. He wants all the water for himself."

"Where is your chief?" asked the man.

"You must follow the brook farther up," they told him.

The man walked on and at last met the big chief. When he saw him he trembled with fright, because the chief was a monster so huge that if one stood at his feet, one could not see his head. The monster filled the whole valley from end to end. He had dug himself a huge hole and dammed it up, so that all the water was in it and none could flow into the stream bed. And he had fouled the water and made it poisonous, so that stinking mists covered its slimy surface.

The monster had a mile-wide grinning mouth going from ear to ear. His dull yellow eyes started out of his head like huge pine knots. His body was bloated and covered with warts as big as mountains.

The monster stared dully at the man with his protruding eyes and finally said in a fearsome croak, "Little man, what do you want?"

Lac des Piles, Quebec

The man was terrified, but said: "I come from a village far downstream. Our only spring ran dry because you're keeping all the water for yourself. We would like you to let us have some of this water. Also, please don't muddy it so much."

The monster blinked at him a few times. Finally he croaked:

> *"Do as you please,*
> *Do as you please,*
> *I don't care,*
> *I don't care,*
> *If you want water,*
> *If you want water,*
> *Go elsewhere!"*

The man said, "We need the water. The people are dying of thirst." The monster replied:

> *"I don't care,*
> *I don't care,*
> *Don't bother me,*
> *Don't bother me,*
> *Go away,*
> *Go away,*
> *Or I'll swallow you up!"*

The monster opened his mouth wide from ear to ear, and inside it the man could see the many things that the creature had killed.

The monster gulped a few times and smacked his lips with a noise like thunder. At this the man's courage broke, and he turned and ran away as fast as he could.

Back at his village the man told the people: "Nothing can be done. If we complain, this monster will swallow us up. He'll kill us all."

The people were in despair. "What shall we do?" they cried. Now, Glooscap knows everything that goes on in the world, even before it happens. He sees everything with his inward eye. He said, "I must set things right. I'll have to get water for the people!"

Then Glooscap girded himself for war. He painted his body with paint as red as blood. He made himself twelve feet tall. He used two huge clamshells for his earrings. He put a hundred black eagle feathers and a hundred white eagle feathers in his scalp lock. He painted yellow rings around his eyes. He twisted his mouth into a snarl and made himself look ferocious.

He stamped, and the earth trembled. He uttered his fearful war cry, and it echoed and re-echoed from all the mountains. He grasped a huge mountain in his hand, a mountain composed of flint, and from it made himself a single knife sharp as a weasel's teeth. "Now I am going," he said, striding forth among thunder and lightning, with mighty eagles circling above him.

Thus Glooscap came to the village of the people with the webbed hands and feet.

"I want water," he told them. Looking at him, they were afraid. They brought him a little muddy water. "I think I'll get more and cleaner water," he said. Glooscap went upstream and confronted the monster. "I want clean water," he said, "a lot of it, for the people downstream."

> *"Ho! Ho!*
> *Ho! Ho!*
> *All the waters are mine!*
> *All the waters are mine!*
> *Go away!*
> *Go away!*
> *Or I'll kill you!"*

"Slimy lump of mud!" cried Glooscap. "We'll see who will be killed!"

They fought. The mountains shook. The earth split open. The swamp smoked and burst into flames. Mighty trees were shivered into splinters.

The monster opened its huge mouth wide to swallow Glooscap. Glooscap made himself taller than the tallest tree, and even the monster's mile-wide mouth was too small for him. Glooscap then seized his great flint knife and slit the monster's bloated belly. From the wound gushed a mighty stream, a roaring river, tumbling, rolling, foaming down, down, down, gouging out for itself a vast, deep bed, flowing by the village and on to the great sea of the east.

"That should be enough water for the people," said Glooscap.

He grasped the monster and squeezed him in his mighty palm. He squeezed and squeezed and threw him away, flinging him into the swamp. Glooscap had squeezed this great creature into a small bullfrog, and ever since, the bullfrog's skin has been wrinkled because Glooscap squeezed so hard.

The Origin of the Thunderbird

This is a legend of long ago times. Two Indians desired to find the origin of thunder. They traveled north and came to high mountains. These mountains performed magically. They drew apart, back and forth, then closed together very quickly.

One Indian said, "I will leap through the cleft before it closes. If I am caught, you continue to find the origin of thunder."

The first one succeeded in going through the cleft before it closed, but the second one was caught and squashed.

On the other side, the first Indian saw a large plain with a group of wigwams, and a number of Indians playing a ball game. After a little while, these players said to each other, "It is time to go." They disappeared into their wigwams to put on wings, and came out with their bows and arrows and flew away over the mountains to the south. This was how the Passamaquoddy Indian discovered the homes of the thunderbirds.

The remaining old men of that tribe asked the Passamaquoddy Indian, "What do you want? Who are you?" He replied with the story of his mission. The old men deliberated how they could help him.

They decided to put the lone Indian into a large mortar, and they pounded him until all his bones were broken. They molded him into a new body with wings like thunderbird, and gave him a bow and some arrows and sent him away in flight. They warned him not to fly close to trees, because he flew so fast he could not stop in time to avoid them and he would be killed.

Blue Mountain Lake,
Adirondacks, New York

The lone Indian could not reach his home because the huge enemy bird, Wochowsen, at that time made such a damaging wind. Thunderbird is an Indian, and he or his lightning would never harm another Indian. But Wochowsen, great bird from the south, tried hard to rival thunderbird. So Passamaquoddies feared Wochowsen, whose wings Glooscap once had broken because he used too much power.

A result was that for a long time air became stagnant, the sea was full of slime, and all the fish died. But Glooscap saw what was happening to his people and repaired the wings of Wochowsen to the extent of controlling and alternating strong winds with calm.

Legend tells us this is how the new Passamaquoddy thunderbird, the lone Indian who passed through the cleft, in time became the great and powerful Thunderbird, who always has kept a watchful eye upon the good Indians.

Adirondacks, New York

The First Medicine Man

This is a legend of long ago about a Passamaquoddy woman who traveled constantly back and forth through the woods. From every bush she came to, she bit off a twig, and from one of these she became pregnant. She grew bigger until at last she could no longer travel, at which time she built a wigwam near the mouth of a fresh-running stream.

The woman gave birth during the night. At first, she thought that she should kill her baby. Instead, she made a bark canoe into which she placed her child, then set it adrift downstream. Though the water was sometimes rough, the child was never harmed or even became wet.

The canoe finally reached an Indian village, running aground in front of a group of wigwams. A woman found the baby and brought it to her home.

Every morning thereafter a baby died in the village. The villagers could not figure out what was happening to their children.

A neighbor noticed that the rescued child toddled off to the river every night only to return shortly after. The neighbor wondered if this could have anything to do with the rash of deaths. Then she saw the rescued child return to its wigwam with a small tongue, which it roasted and ate before laying down to sleep.

The next morning, people were alarmed to learn that yet another baby had died. The neighbor was then certain that she knew who the killer was. She informed the parents of the dead child and found out that the dead baby's tongue had been cut out, causing the child to bleed to death.

The villagers deliberated as to what to do with the murderer. Some said cut up the culprit and throw him into the river. Others said to burn the cut up pieces, which was the side that prevailed.

After cutting up the rescued child, they torched the fragments, letting them burn until there was nothing left but ashes.

Everyone assumed that this was the end of it. However, to the villagers' dismay, the child returned like before with a small tongue, which it roasted and ate. Unsurprisingly, another baby was reported dead the next morning. When the villagers confronted the resurrected child, the child declared that he would never kill any more children, for he had become grown.

As a demonstration of his more mature status, the boy began to take a bone out of his side, which led to all of his bones spilling out of his body into a pile on the ground. The boy then drew his fingers across his eyes and closed them. Without bones, the boy could not move and became very fat over time.

To the villagers' surprise, the boy became a great medicine man. Anything the people desired within reason was granted to them. One day, though, the villagers decided to move on. But before they left, they built a fine wigwam for the medicine man. Everyone had become accustomed to turning to him with their requests. When he granted their wishes, he asked them, "Turn me over and you will find your medicine beneath me."

A young man wanted the love of a woman. "Turn me over," said the medicine man. The young man did and found an herb. "You must not give this away or throw it away," said the medicine man. With these instructions and the herb, the young man returned home.

It was not long, though, before the young man discovered that many women wanted to keep him company. So many in fact that the young man soon became tired of all the attention. Feeling overwhelmed by the herb's unexpected results, the young man gave it back to the medicine man.

On another occasion another man wanted to live as long as the world shall stand. "Your request is a hard one to consider," replied the medicine man, "but I will do my best to answer it."

Upon turning the medicine man over, the man found an herb. "Go to a place that is bare of everything," the medicine man instructed, "so bare it is destitute of all vegetation, and just stand there."

The man went in the direction that the medicine man pointed to. As he did, the man looked back at the medicine man, who began sprouting twigs and branches all over his body. Eventually, the medicine man turned into a cedar tree, which he would be forever—useless to everyone.

Adirondacks, New York

5

LEGENDS & LANDS FROM THE NORTHWEST

The region of the Northwest stretches in a long, narrow coastal strip from Alaska down to northern California. Its terrain is marked by mountain ranges, islands, and coastal inlets. The Northwest Pacific coast enjoys abundant rainfall and lush forests with dense foliage and large trees. The greenery in this northern rainforest blocks out much of the sunlight, which creates a dark, moist environment teeming with mosses and ferns. The Pacific Ocean and numerous rivers and lakes provided local American Indian tribes, such as the Nootka, Kwakiutl, Salish, and Quillayute, ample fish and game. Along with elk, antelope, bear, and deer, they feasted on salmon and other fish.

Lands of the American Indians of the Northwest

Plentiful food sustained a dense population while dense forests supplied materials for boats and shelters. The land and water's natural abundance and the ease these peoples had in obtaining necessities, afforded them the time and luxury to create an affluent and elaborately structured society. The custom of the potlatch, in which an individual's prestige corresponded to his material wealth and ability to give away many of his possessions, was common.

Most homes were built close to the water, often on beaches. Because of the difficulty imposed by traveling through the inland mountainous terrain, most American Indians preferred to travel and trade by boat or canoe on the lakes, rivers, and coastal waters. Natives built wooden houses and constructed tall, carved wooden totem poles as well as wooden boxes, chests, and masks.

When the Animals and Birds Were Created

When the world was very young, there were no people on the earth. There were no birds or animals either. There was nothing but grass and sand and creatures that were neither animals nor people but had some of the traits of people and some of the traits of animals.

Then the two brothers of the Sun and the Moon came to the earth. Their names were *Ho-ho-e-ap-bess*, which means "The Two-Men-Who-Changed-Things." They came to make the earth ready for a new race of people, the Indians. The Two-Men-Who-Changed-Things called all the creatures to them. Some they changed into animals and birds. Some they changed into trees and smaller plants.

Among them was a bad thief. He was always stealing food from creatures who were fishermen and hunters. The Two-Men-Who-Changed-Things transformed him into Seal. They shortened his arms and tied his legs so that only his feet could move. Then they threw Seal into the Ocean and said to him, "Now you will have to catch your own fish if you are to have anything to eat."

One of the creatures was a great fisherman. He was always on the rocks or was wading with his long fishing spear. He kept it ready to thrust into some fish. He always wore a little cape, round and white, over his shoulders. The Two-Men-Who-Changed-Things transformed him into Great Blue Heron. The long fishing spear became his sharp-pointed bill.

Another creature was both a fisherman and a thief. He had stolen a necklace of shells. The Two-Men-Who-Changed-Things

PAGE 128: Nimpkish Burial Grounds, Alert Bay, British Columbia

RIGHT: Vargas Island Park, British Columbia

Seals, Olympic Peninsula, Washington

transformed him into
Kingfisher. The necklace of
shells was turned into a ring of
feathers around Kingfisher's
neck. He is still a fisherman.
He watches the water, and
when he sees a fish, he dives
headfirst with a splash into the
water.

Two creatures had huge
appetites. They devoured everything they could find. The Two-
Men-Who-Changed-Things
transformed one of them into
Raven. They transformed his
wife into Crow. Both Raven
and Crow were given strong
beaks so that they could
tear their food. Raven croaks
"Crrruck!" and Crow answers
with a loud "Cah! Cah!"

The Two-Men-Who-
Changed-Things called
Bluejay's son to them and
asked, "Which do you wish to
be—a bird or a fish?"

"I don't want to be either,"
he answered.

"Then we will transform you
into Mink. You will live on
land. You will eat the fish you
can catch from the water or
can pick up on the shore."

Then the Two-Men-Who-Changed-Things remembered that the new people would need wood for many things.

They called one of the creatures to them and said, "The Indians will want tough wood to make bows with. They will want tough wood to make wedges with, so that they can split logs. You are tough and strong. We will change you into the yew tree."

They called some little creatures to them. "The new people will need many slender, straight shoots for arrows. You will be the arrowwood. You will be white with many blossoms in early summer."

They called a big, fat creature to them. "The Indians will need big trunks with soft wood so that they can make canoes. You will be the cedar trees. The Indians will make many things from your bark and from your roots."

The Two-Men-Who-Changed-Things knew that the Indians would need wood for fuel. So they called an old creature to them. "You are old and your heart is dry. You will make good kindling because your grease has turned hard and will make pitch. You will be the spruce tree. When you grow old you will always make dry wood that will be good for fires."

To another creature they said, "You shall be the hemlock. Your bark will be good for tanning hides. Your branches will be used in the sweat lodges."

A creature with a cross temper they changed into a crab apple tree, saying, "You will always bear sour fruit."

Another creature they changed into the wild cherry tree, so that the new people would have fruit and could use the cherry bark for medicine.

A thin, tough creature they changed into the alder tree, so that the new people would have hard wood for their canoe paddles.

Thus the Two-Men-Who-Changed-Things got the world ready for the new people who were to come. They made the world as *it* was when the Indians lived in it.

Wakiash and the First Totem Pole

It happened once among the Kwakiutl that the whole tribe was having a dance. Wakiash, a chief, had never created a dance of his own. He was unhappy because all the other chiefs had fine dances. So he thought, "I will go up into the mountains to fast, and perhaps a dance will come to me."

Wakiash made himself ready and went to the mountains, where he stayed, fasting and bathing, for four days. Early in the morning of the fourth day, he grew so weary that he laid down on his back and fell asleep. Suddenly, he felt something on his chest and awoke to find a little green frog.

"Lie still," the frog said, "because you're on the back of a raven who's going to fly us around the world. Then you may see what you want and take it." The raven began beating its wings; then they flew off for four days. Wakiash saw many things during his flight. But it was when they were on their way back that Wakiash saw what he really wanted: a house with a beautiful totem pole out front and the sound of singing inside. The frog knew Wakiash's thoughts, so the raven was asked to coast to the ground. The frog then told Wakiash to hide behind the door of the house.

"When they begin to dance," the frog said, "leap into the room."

The people inside, however, were unable to begin either dancing or singing. "Something's the matter," one of them said. "There must be something near us that's causing this." The chief agreed and said, "Someone who can run fast should go see what it is."

Just then a tiny mouse volunteered to investigate the problem. At the time, though, the mouse had taken off her mouse-skin and was in the form of a woman. In fact, everyone in the house had taken off their animal skins for the dance and was standing in human form.

Becoming a mouse again, the woman whisked outside to see what was stopping their dance. Wakiash caught her though and gave her some mountain goat's fat. The mouse was pleased with her gift and began talking with Wakiash.

"What do you want?" she asked.

"I wish for the house, the totem pole, and dances inside," Wakiash answered.

"Wait here," the mouse said. "Wait till I come again."

With that the mouse returned inside to tell her friends that she could not find anything. They tried dancing three more times. But each time it was the same thing, so they sent the mouse out to investigate. Each time Wakiash fed the mouse fat, and the mouse returned to say that she saw nothing.

Finally, on the fourth attempt, after the mouse reported there was nothing, they began dancing again. At that moment, Wakiash leapt into the room. All at once the dancers dropped their heads in shame because a man had seen them looking like humans when they were all really animals. Everyone stood silently until at last the mouse said, "We should ask what our friend wants."

They lifted their heads and the chief, who was really a beaver, asked Wakiash what he wanted from them. Wakiash responded with only his thoughts. He wanted the house, the totem pole, and especially the dance, because he had never had one of his own. The mouse then told the rest what Wakiash was thinking. The chief in turn said, "Let our friend sit down. We'll show him how we dance, and he can choose whichever dances he likes."

Everyone began dancing again, then after a long evening, the chief asked Wakiash which dances he liked. What impressed Wakiash the most were the wonderful masks that the dancers used. Wakiash wanted the Echo mask and the mask of the Little Man who goes around the house talking a lot and trying to argue with everyone. As Wakiash formed his thoughts, the mouse relayed them to the chief. Before the night was over Wakiash saw all of the dances, and he was encouraged to take as many as he pleased, along with the house and the totem pole.

Nimpkish Burial Grounds, Alert Bay, British Columbia

The chief, keeping his promise to Wakiash, folded everything up into a little bundle and gave it to Wakiash. "When you reach home," the chief said, "throw down this bundle. The house and everything else will become like you saw them here."

Wakiash went back to the raven, and the raven flew back toward the mountain where their journey began. Before they arrived Wakiash fell asleep. When he awoke, the raven and the frog were gone, and he was alone.

It was night by the time Wakiash returned to his village. He threw down the bundle and the house and totem pole appeared! The whale painted on the house was blowing. The animals carved on the totem pole were making their noises. And all the masks inside the house were talking and crying.

The commotion woke up Wakiash's people, so they all came to see what was happening. What they found was Wakiash, who, to Wakiash's surprise, had not been gone four days but for four years. Happy to see Wakiash again, everyone entered the house and Wakiash began making his dance. Wakiash demonstrated the masks along with teaching the people all the new songs and dances. When they finally stopped dancing, the house disappeared. It went back to the animals.

Wakiash, though, had learned much from the animals. He made a house, totem pole, and masks from wood. The totem pole was the first of its kind, and the people made a song for it. The animals, they learned from Wakiash, called the totem pole Kalakuyuwish, "the pole that holds up the sky." The totem pole was so tall and heavy that it made a creaking noise. In the end, Wakiash took for his name that of the totem pole, Kalakuyuwish.

Nimpkish Burial Grounds, Alert Bay, British Columbia

Raven and Crow's Potlatch

Raven used to live high up in the upper Skagit River country. He was very lazy. In the summer when the other animals were busy gathering food for winter, Raven would be flying from rock to stump and back again, making fun of them. Raven just laughed when his cousin Crow urged him to follow Squirrel's example. But Raven never prepared for the cold months before the snow covered the ground and the remaining food.

Raven soon found himself in trouble. The snows were deep and Raven was hungry. Raven's only hope was to find someone willing to share his food with him.

Raven went to see Squirrel. He had a huge supply of nuts and seeds hidden all over the place. Raven poked his head into the dray Squirrel had made in an old fir tree. Politely, Raven begged for some food, to which Squirrel responded by scolding Raven. "You refused to work and save for winter!" Squirrel snapped. "You poked much fun at me. You deserve to starve!"

Raven went to see Bear. However, Bear was sound asleep in his den and could not be wakened. Raven looked around for some food, but it was all in Bear's stomach. Bear had eaten it all and would not be up again until spring.

Raven was becoming hungrier. "Who can give me something to eat?" he wondered sadly. "Everyone is either stingy like Squirrel or asleep like Bear, or else they have flown south for the winter like the Geese." Then Raven suddenly remembered Crow—he would be easy to fool!

Raven flew to Crow's nest. "Cousin Crow, we must talk about your upcoming potlatch."

"I'm not planning any potlatch," Crow replied.

"Crow, everyone is talking about your potlatch," Raven said, ignoring Crow. "Will you sing?"

"Sing?" Crow said, surprised that anyone was interested in his singing when they had never been before.

"You're very talented, cousin," said Raven. "Everyone will be disappointed if you don't sing."

"What potlatch?" Crow exclaimed. "Do you really like my singing?"

"We love your singing," Raven answered. "You'll help us forget about how cold and hungry we are. Now get started preparing the food. I'll invite all the guests. You can practice your singing while you work."

Crow finally gave in and began all the preparations. The more he prepared, the more excited Crow became, especially about singing.

Meanwhile, Raven was inviting all the animals of the forest—except for Squirrel, of course. "Come to *my* potlatch," he told them. Raven went on to exclaim all the delicious food they would all enjoy, in addition to Crow's singing.

Crow was busy singing and cooking when Raven returned. "Everyone is coming," Raven told Crow. "Be sure to prepare all your food! Most of all, keep practicing those wonderful songs."

As the guests arrived, Raven welcomed them to *his* potlatch. The guests were seated and the feast was brought out. Crow was seating himself, when Raven asked him for a song. Flattered, Crow began to sing. After each song, Raven implored Crow for another. The guests also encouraged Crow to keep singing as they filled themselves on Crow's food. Eventually, after singing day and night, Crow's voice became very hoarse until Crow was going "Caw! Caw!" like he does today.

Totem pole, Duncan, British Columbia

As was the custom, the guests, including Raven, packed up all the leftovers and took them to their respective homes. Crow was left with nothing to eat and all of the cleaning up to do. "At least," Crow thought, "I won't go hungry. They'll invite me to their potlatches." But the invitations never came. Since Raven told everyone that it was his potlatch, he was the one who got invited everywhere, keeping his stomach full for several winters.

Because Crow had been so badly fooled, he was reduced to starving, plus he never regained his old singing voice. Instead, Crow was made to go scavenging for scraps of food, forever shouting "Caw! Caw! Caw!"

Hoh Rain Forest, Olympic National Park, Washington

Origin of the Gnawing Beaver

There was a great hunter ever on the alert for new territories. He would go away by himself for long periods of time and return with many furs and a lot of food. Although he was wealthy, he remained single despite his family begging him to take a wife. Instead he simply observed all the fasts of cleanliness for hunters and stayed away from women.

But one day after a hunting trip, he decided, "I will take a wife now. I will then move far away, where I hear that game is plentiful." He then married a young woman from a neighboring village, who, like him, appreciated the hunting ways.

After a while, the hunter and his wife moved to a faraway place, where he built a house, and they enjoyed each other's company every night. From there the hunter began going away to hunt in new territories. He would always be away for two or three nights. When he returned, it was with many furs and much meat. The hunter's wife was always happy to see her husband return, as she spotted his canoe before dark.

While the hunter was away, his wife amused herself by going to a stream near their home. She bathed and swam in a pool. She was quite content. So her husband said to her one day, "Since you've become used to being alone, I'm going on a longer trip."

While her husband was away this time, his wife grew weary of the small pool in which she swam. So she built a dam, turning the pool into a lake. Soon she was spending all her time swimming and bathing. Her husband was happy to see what she had done upon his return. Once again, though, he decided to go on an even longer trip.

While the hunter was away this time, his wife built a little house of mud and branches at the lake. After swimming all day, she enjoyed resting in her little home. At first she would sleep in her husband's lodge at night, but eventually she grew more accustomed to her mud-and-branches house at the lake. Though she was now pregnant, she was uncomfortable staying with her husband in their lodge. She wanted instead to keep more to herself.

The hunter continued with his hunting trips. To pass the time, the hunter's wife enlarged the lake by building her dam higher. She constructed another dam downstream, then another. Soon she had a number of small lakes all connected to the large one in which she had her lodge.

When the hunter returned from his latest and longest trip he could not find his wife. He spent several days and nights looking for her, but to no avail. He even went around the lake that she had created with her dam, but nothing. Eventually he became convinced that something serious had happened to his wife. He had wanted to return to their home village, but knew that he could not without his wife. He began singing a dirge.

As the hunter sang and cried, a figure emerged from the lake. It was a strange animal with a stick in its mouth that it gnawed. On either side of this animal were two smaller ones, also gnawing on sticks. The larger one, wearing a hat shaped like a gnawed stick, spoke to the hunter, saying, "Don't be so sad. It is I, your wife, and your two children. We have returned to our home in the water. Now that you have seen me, you will use me as a crest. Call me the Woman-Beaver and the crest Remnants-of-Chewing-Stick. The children are First Beaver, and you will refer to them as the Offspring of Woman-Beaver." Woman-Beaver then disappeared into the water, and the hunter saw her no more.

At once the hunter packed up his belongings, loaded the canoe, then headed down river to his village. After returning home, the hunter did not speak to his people for a long time. Finally, he told them what had happened. "I will take this as my personal crest," the hunter declared. "It shall be known as Remnants-of-Chewing-Stick, and forever remain the property of our clan, the Salmon-Eater household." This is the origin of the Beaver crest and the Remnants-of-Chewing-Stick.

Alert Bay, Cormorant Channel
Marine Park, British Columbia

Creation of the Animal People

The earth was once a human being. Old-One made her out of a woman. "You will be the mother of all people," he said.

Earth is alive yet, but she has been changed. The soil is her flesh. The rocks are her bones. The wind is her breath. The trees and grass are her hair. When she moves, we have an earthquake.

After changing her to earth, Old-One took some of her flesh and rolled it into balls. Old-One then turned these balls of soil into the beings of the early world. They were people, yet at the same time animals. Some could fly like birds, while others could swim like the fish. They all had the gift of speech. In many ways, they were much smarter than the people and animals of today. On the other hand, they were also much stupider. They knew that they needed to hunt in order to live, but they did not know what to hunt.

Something like people lived on the earth, similar to the Indians, only ignorant. There were also deer, elk, and antelope, who some say were always in their animal forms since the beginning. There are many stories about them.

The balls of mud Old-One made were almost all alike and were different from the first ones he made. He rolled them over and over. He shaped them like Indians. He blew on them and they became alive. Old-One called them men. They were Indian, but they did not know anything, like children. In fact, because they were helpless, some of the other creatures preyed on them.

Old-One made both male and female people and animals, so that they could breed and multiply. They would bear fruit and grow like the plants and trees of the forest. Unfortunately, most of the ancient animal people were selfish, creating much trouble among themselves. Old-One said of this, "There will soon be no people if I let things go on like this."

So Old-One sent Coyote to kill all the monsters and other evil things. Old-One told Coyote to teach the Indians the best way of doing things and the best way of making things. Life would be easier and better for them when they were no longer ignorant. Coyote then traveled on the earth and did many wonderful things.

Roosevelt elk, Olympic National Park, Washington

How Raven Helped the Ancient People

Long ago, near the beginning of the world, Gray Eagle was the guardian of the sun, moon, and stars as well as the fresh water and fire. Gray Eagle hated people, though, so much so that he kept everything under his protection hidden from them. Consequently, people lived in darkness, with no fresh water or fire.

Gray Eagle had a beautiful daughter with whom Raven fell in love. At the time, Raven was a handsome young man. He changed himself into a snow-white bird, which pleased Gray Eagle's daughter. So she invited him to her father's lodge.

When Raven saw all that Gray Eagle kept hidden, he knew what he had to do. He watched for his chance to take them when no one was looking. When that chance came, Raven grabbed the sun, moon, and stars, as well as the fresh water and a brand of fire. Raven then escaped through the smoke hole of Gray Eagle's lodge.

As soon as Raven got outside, he hung the sun up in the sky. It cast so much light that Raven was able to fly out to an island in the middle of the ocean. When the sun set, he fastened the moon in the sky and dispersed the stars in different places. By this new light Raven kept on flying, carrying with him the fresh water and the brand of fire.

Raven flew back over the land. When he reached the right place, he dropped all the water to the ground. When the fresh water fell it became the source of many streams and lakes. Then Raven flew on, still holding the brand of fire in his bill. The smoke from the fire blew back over Raven's white feathers. When his bill began to burn after carrying the firebrand for so long, he had to let it go. It struck rocks and went into them. That is why if you strike two rocks together sparks fly out.

Raven's feathers never turned white again after carrying the firebrand. That is why Raven is now a black bird.

Olympic Coast National Marine Sanctuary, Quileute Indian Reservation, Washington

Coyote's Salmon

Long ago on the Sanpoil River that flows southward into the Columbia River, Old Man and Old Woman lived with their tribe the Sanpoils. A very pretty granddaughter lived with them.

Coyote came along one day and saw the little family. Instantly, Coyote fell in love with the granddaughter. He knew that he had to take her as his wife. So Coyote began his pursuit of her by ingratiating himself to her grandparents.

Old Man and Old Woman could not help but notice how striking Coyote looked. His long hair was neatly braided and his forelocks were carefully combed back. He was also very tall and strong. They wondered if he was a chief.

Eventually, Coyote asked Old Man, "What's that thing down in the stream?"

"Why, that's my fish trap," replied Old Man.

"A fish trap? What's that? What do you do with it?" Coyote pretended not to know.

"Oh, occasionally I catch a few bullheads and sunfish with it," Old Man said.

"I've never heard of them. Are they very big?" asked Coyote.

"They're not much, but we have nothing else to eat around here," Old Man replied.

Just before sunset Coyote told Old Man, "I think that I'll go up the hill and look around." While he was out and about, Coyote found five grouse that he killed by throwing stones at them. He then took his kill back to Old Man and said, "Let's eat these." They wound up having a wonderful meal.

"Do you eat this kind of food everyday?" Old Man asked Coyote.

"Sometimes I eat berries and roots. And sometimes I'll catch fish as long as your arm," replied Coyote. Old Man nodded his head.

Later that night, Coyote finally told Old Man and Old Woman that he wished to marry their granddaughter. Coyote then left the lodge, asking them to think about his proposal. Once he left the room, Old Man wondered whether or not accepting Coyote as a son-in-law would mean that they would get to eat as well as tonight all the time. "Well, husband," Old Woman said, "I'll leave it entirely up to you."

Coyote returned. He sat next to Old Man, who was holding his pipe to his mouth, quietly wishing for some tobacco. "Have some of mine," Coyote said, handing over a large bunch of tobacco.

Coyote and Old Man then discussed Coyote's proposal, and after assuring Old Man that he would be able to take good care of his granddaughter, Old Man gave his consent. Coyote took the pretty granddaughter for his wife.

Coyote was very pleased with his new family. One day he told his wife that he was going downstream, but that he would be back a little later. "All right," his wife said.

What Coyote did was change Old Man's fish trap into a basket-type trap, piling rows of rocks to guide fish into the basket. When he finished reworking the trap, he said, "Salmon, I want two of you in the basket trap tomorrow morning, one male and one female." Then he returned home.

The next day, Coyote told Old Man that he thought he heard something downstream where his trap was; maybe he should take

Glaucous-winged gull,
Goldstream Provincial Park,
British Columbia

a look. After breakfast, Old Man went downstream to investigate. What he found were two large fish. Excited, he rushed back to Coyote to tell him the good news.

"You must be dreaming," said Coyote. "Come and see for yourself," replied Old Man.

When they arrived at the fish trap, sure enough, there were two of the biggest salmon they ever saw.

"You're right!" Coyote exclaimed. "These are indeed salmon, king of the fish. Let's take these over to that flat area over there, and I'll show you what to do with them."

Old Man followed along and watched. The first thing Coyote did was spread sunflower plants on the ground, on which he placed the two salmon. Coyote then demonstrated how to prepare the salmon.

"First, put a stick in the salmon's mouth and bend it back to break off the head. Second, place long sharp poles inside the salmon lengthwise to hold for roasting over your campfire.

"Now remember this. The first week go down to the trap and take out the salmon everyday. But when fixing it, never use a knife to cut it in any way. Always roast the fish over a fire on sticks, the

Lake Crescent, Olympic National Park, Washington

way I have shown you. Never boil salmon the first week. After the salmon is roasted, open it carefully and take out the backbone without breaking it. Also, save the back part of the head for the sacred bundle—never eat that.

"If you do not do these things as I have told you, either a big storm will come up and you will be drowned, or you will be bitten by a rattlesnake and you will die.

"After you have taken out the salmon's backbone, wrap it and the back of the head carefully in tules, the marsh grasses, to make a sacred bundle, then place it somewhere in a tree, where it will not be bothered. If you do as I tell you, you will always have plenty of salmon in your trap.

"I am telling you these sacred things about the salmon because I am going to die sometime. I want you and your tribe to know the best way to care for and use your salmon. After this, your men will always place their fish traps up and down the river to catch salmon. The man having the first trap will be Chief of the Salmon, and the others should always do anything that he tells them to do.

"After the first week of the salmon season, you can boil your salmon or cook it any way you wish. But remember to always take care of the bones, wrapping them in a sacred bundle—never leaving them where they can be stepped upon or stepped over." With that, Coyote finished all that he had to say to Old Man about the salmon.

Old Man followed Coyote's instructions and found that his salmon yield was increasing all the time. Over the weeks, people eventually noticed how well Old Man and Old Woman were doing. Soon word spread about the bounty of big red fish and the tall stranger who taught Old Man how to trap them. People came to see for themselves.

Old Man and Old Woman invited their neighbors to feast on the salmon. They then told everyone everything they had learned from their Coyote son-in-law. To this day, the Sanpoils claim that they harvest salmon in exactly the same way that Coyote taught their ancestors long ago.

The Northern Lights and Creatures of the Sky

The northern lights come from the fires of a tribe of dwarf Indians who live a long way to the north. These dwarfs are no taller than half the length of a canoe paddle. They live on the ice and they eat seals and whales. Although they are small, they are very strong and hardy. They can dive into freezing water and catch whales with their hands. They then take the whale and boil out the blubber over fires they build on the ice. These fires are the northern lights.

The stars overhead are Indian spirits, as well as the spirits of animals, birds, and fish. Comets and meteors are the spirits of departed chiefs.

The rainbow is associated with the Thunderbird in some way. The rainbow is armed with powerful claws at each end of its bow shape, with which it will grab anyone who gets too near.

Thunderbird is a giant Indian living on the highest mountain. When he is hungry he wears the head of a giant bird and a pair of giant wings. He covers his body with feathers and ties Lightning Fish around his waist. Lightning Fish have heads as sharp as a knife and red tongues that make fire. It is this way that Thunderbird goes hunting for whales.

When Thunderbird flies toward the ocean, his wings darken the sky, and their flapping makes a huge noise. When he sees a whale, he throws Lightning Fish into its body and kills it. Then he carries the whale back to his mountain home, where he eats it.

Sometimes Thunderbird will miss a whale with his Lightning Fish and strike a tree instead, tearing it to pieces. Sometimes the Lightning Fish will strike a man and kill him. Whatever Lightning Fish strikes on the land has special powers, which the Indians try to recover and keep. Even a piece of the Lightning Fish's bone, which is bright red, will endow the man who finds it with great skill as a whale hunter and in other kinds of works and deeds.

Clayoquot Sound, British Columbia

Thunderbird and Whale

Long ago there was a desperate time in the land of the Quillayute. For endless days a great storm blew across the land. Rain, hail, sleet, and snow came down in droves. The hailstones were so large that they killed many people. The survivors were driven from their coastal home onto the prairie, which was the highest part of their land.

The people grew thin and weak from hunger. The hailstones had beaten down the ferns, camas, and berries. Ice locked the rivers so that men could not fish. Storms rocked the ocean so that fishermen could not go out in their canoes for deep-sea fishing. Soon the people had eaten all the grass and roots on the prairie. There was no food left. The children began dying. The people called on the Great Spirit, but no help seemed forthcoming.

The great chief of the Quillayute called his people to council.

"Take comfort, my people," said the great chief. "We will call again on the Great Spirit for help. If no help comes, then we will know that it is His will that we die here on the prairie. And we will die bravely in the Quillayute way. But first, let us speak with the Great Spirit."

The weak and hungry people sat silently as the great chief spoke to the Great Spirit on their behalf.

When his prayer ended, the chief turned to his people and said, "Now we will wait for the will of the One who is wise and all-powerful."

The people waited. There was nothing but silence and darkness. Suddenly, there came a great noise and flashes of lightning cut through the darkness. Just as suddenly, there was another great noise. Then a deep, whirring sound arose like the beating of massive wings came from the west. Everyone looked toward the sky above as a huge bird-shaped creature flew towards them.

Olympic Coast National Marine Sanctuary, Washington

Larger than anything they had ever seen before, the creature's wings were twice as long as a war canoe. It possessed a huge, curving beak, and its eyes glowed like fire. In its claws the people saw an enormous whale, squirming with life.

They watched in amazement as the Thunderbird, which all the people began calling it, carefully set the whale on the ground before them. Thunderbird then flew into the sky, gave a resounding cry, and returned to the thunder and lightning from which it came. Some thought it flew back to the Great Spirit.

Thunderbird and Whale saved the Quillayute from starvation. The people knew that the Great Spirit had answered their prayer. Even today they never forget what Thunderbird did for them to end their plight. For on the prairie near their village are big, round stones that the old ones say are the hardened hailstones of that long-ago storm.

Olympic Coast National Marine Sanctuary, Quileute Indian Reservation, Washington

The Valley of Peace in the Olympics

Long ago, the Indians had a sacred place in the heart of the Olympic Mountains. It was a valley, wide and level, with high peaks on every side. The base of the mountains was covered with cedar, fir, and pine, which stayed green throughout the year. A small stream murmured through the valley, and many kinds of flowers grew on the banks, spreading into the meadows.

Many neighboring tribes regarded this valley as eminently sacred. Once a year, all the tribes, even those who otherwise made war with each other, gathered in this valley. During this time, they would put away their weapons, go down into the valley and greet their neighbors and former enemies with signs of peace. Instead of fighting, they enjoyed trading and playing games of skill and strength. These annual meetings went on for many years.

However, Seatco, chief of the evil beings, became angry with the people who gathered in the valley. Seatco was a giant who could trample a whole tribe under his feet. He was taller than the tallest fir tree. His voice was louder than the roar of the ocean, and his face was more terrible to look at than the fiercest of beasts. He could easily travel by land, water, or air. He was strong enough to tear up a whole forest by the roots and heap rocks onto the mountains. He could even change the course of a river by simply blowing on it.

For no reason then, Seatco became angry with the tribes that gathered in the valley. One year, when they were there for trading and games, Seatco came among them. He caused the mountains to tremble. The earth split open and swallowed many people. Not many Indians escaped from this rampage. The few who managed to flee rushed back to their villages to warn their people to stay away from the valley. The Indians never went there again.

Hoh Rain Forest, Olympic
National Park, Washington

p.15: Poetry in Paul Zolbrod. *Reading the Voice: Native American Oral Poetry on the Written Page.* (Salt Lake City: University of Utah Press, 1995).

p.16: Rodney Frey (ed.). *Stories That Made the World: Oral Literature of the Indian Peoples of the Inland Northwest.* (Norman: University of Oklahoma Press, 1995).

p.16: Keith H. Basso. *Wisdom Sits in Places: Landscape and Language Among the Western Apache.* (Albuquerque: University of New Mexico Press, 1996).

p.17: A. Irving Hallowell. "Ojibwa Ontology, Behavior, and World View" In *Teachings From the American Earth: Indian Religion and Philosophy.* Dennis Tedlock and Barbara Tedlock (editors). (New York: Liveright, 1992).

p.21: Chief Joseph in Dee Brown. *Bury My Heart at Wounded Knee: An Indian History of the American West.* (New York: Holt, Rinehart & Winston, 1970).

p.23: Christopher Vecsey. *Imagine Ourselves Richly: Mythic Narratives of North American Indians.* (San Francisco: HarperSanFrancisco, 1991).

p.29: George Linden. "Dakota Philosophy," in *The Black Elk Reader.* Clyde Holler (editor). (Syracuse: Syracuse University Press, 2000).

About the Author

David Martínez, Ph.D., is a professor of American Indian Studies at the University of Minnesota, where he teaches courses in American Indian philosophies. Dr. Martínez, the son of a Mexican-American father and Pima mother, was born in Phoenix, Arizona, near the Gila River Pima Indian Community and was reared in the working-class neighborhood of Pomona, California, near Los Angeles. Realizing the wealth of ideas and values American Indians have held, Dr. Martínez pursued a unique philosophical approach to American Indian religious traditions while earning a B.A. in philosophy from the University of Rhode Island and a doctorate in philosophy from the State University of New York at Stony Brook. He has also received an M.A. from the American Indian Studies Program at the University of Arizona. Since 1990, Dr. Martínez has been awarded many fellowships and has published articles on American Indian philosophies, aesthetics, and religion in academic journals and quarterlies, such as International Studies in Philosophy, Blackwell, *and the* American Indian Philosophical Association Newsletter. *He lives in Minneapolis with his wife Sharon.*

About the Photographer

Elan Penn is a publisher and photographer with a special interest in books that depict the cultural and natural heritage of people from different parts of the world. Look for his pictorial works, From Sea to Shining Sea: Places That Shaped America *(Sterling, 2003),* The Legends & Lands of Ireland *(Sterling, 2003), and* Between Heaven & Earth: Testimonies to 2,000 Years of Christianity in the Holy Land *(Penn Publishing, 2004).*

Index